Run Gently, Run Long

by Joe Henderson

Illustrations by Bil Canfield
Cover photo by Stan Pantovic

© 1974 by
Runner's World Magazine

World Publications

Post Office Box 366
Mountain View, California 94040

CONTENTS

FOREWORD

796.4
H46r
1974

"The man who is always trying to win can never win,
while the one who does not strive for victory
but is satisfied with his lot
is always a winner."

— **Lao Tzu**

"The highway is for gamblers
better use your sense.
Take what you have gathered
from coincidence."

— **Bob Dylan**

The Chinese philosopher and the American song-poet are worlds apart in time and space.

Lao-Tzu wrote more than 20 centuries ago, synthesizing the oriental wisdom that had developed before him and carrying it on to the generations that followed. The words have lasted.

Bob Dylan rolled in and out with the wave of folksingers of the 1960s. The singers and their songs came and went as quickly as the first breath of spring, and, in the words of one, their voices, were quickly scattered by the swirling winds of time and changing tastes. Dylan was the pop prophet of a time when no one seemed to listen and where nothing lasted long.

I use the words of the modern Western singer and the ancient Chinese teacher to start the book, because this is a book about fleeting things and lasting things, about letting go of one and holding to the other, and about telling which is which.

Racing success is fleeting. It comes and goes quickly, if at all. A runner must see that trying to hold onto this success is as futile as trying to hold back the water or the wind, the sun or the seasons.

Running itself, though—the everyday doing it and feeling good about doing it and wanting to do more of it for thousands of to-morrows—can be as lasting as anything in this life. In this throw-away world, we need lasting things.

This book is a little about racing success and how to achieve it, but it's mostly about running longevity and how to last. It talks about the same things I talked about in *LSD—The Humane Way to Train* five years earlier. But this is not *LSD Revisited*. I'm not here to praise the name LSD but to bury it in favor of a new definition, one that fills in the holes and corrects the wrong ideas left by the first one.

I've made mistakes in my running the last several years—costly, painful mistakes that almost ended running for me. But pain is been a good teacher recently, same as it was in 1966 when I first turned to LSD.

I'm writing from my "experiment of one." The examples are mine. In that way, the book is self-centered. But I write this way only because I know myself best. The principles involved are universal and they'll outlast me. My experiences are fleeting, and I don't care if you forget them the minute after you've read those chapters. But try to hold onto the lasting principles.

This is not a comparative scientific treatment of gentle, long-lasting running. I know the scientific basis for it, but that's a discussion for another book, another time. Here, I don't give anything more than a personal accounting of experiences. These experiences add up not to a method of training but to a philosophy of running, a way of looking at the activity. It isn't the way everyone should look at it. I don't ask everyone to be like me. It doesn't fit some personalities. But it offers a good alternative for those who've raced themselves dry and are looking for a change.

I know from my own years in the sport that the best preparation for racing isn't always—or even often—best for a runner's health and longevity. This doesn't mean stop racing or race with only half a heart. It means balancing racing ambitions against a view to the distant future, pacing the running for the long haul.

This is not a step-by-step guide to specifics of running gently and running long. There are no schedules as such, because that would tie you to my plan instead of freeing you to find your own.

An old proverb says you do a man no favors when you give him a fish. He eats it and it's gone, and he's soon hungry again. But show him *how to fish* for himself and he'll never be hungry.

By painting broad patterns and leaving the details to you, I'm trying to show you one way of fishing. It isn't an original way, but I never claimed it as my invention. There are contradictions in what I say, perhaps, but a philosophy doesn't come equipped with the same consistency as a scientific method.

Critics will pick holes in what I say. That's okay. I'm not writing to anwer or please critics, but to encourage those of you who want to listen.

The End

BEYOND FIT AND FAST

Jonathan Livingston Seagull caught a fresh vision of what flying could be. It wasn't practical and it wasn't popular with fellow gulls, but Jonathan didn't mind. He went ahead and chased his vision anyway.

Richard Bach turned the story of that chase into a best-selling little novel named after the main character. On the surface, it's a simple tale of a bird and his troubles. But it isn't really about birds at all. Bach dedicates the book "to the real Jonathan Seagull, who lives within us all."

It is a book about people who say that liking what they do is reason enough for doing it.

J. L. Seagull liked to fly. Flying was his passion, and he wanted it to be more than "flapping around from place to place. A... a... *mosquito* does that!"

Bach wrote, "Most gulls don't bother to learn more than the simplest facts of flight—how to get from shore to food and back again. For most gulls, it is not flying that matters, but eating. For this gull, though, it was not eating that mattered, but flight. More than anything else, Jonathan Livingston Seagull loved to fly."

Conventional gulls in the flock decided Jonathan was giving too much time and attention to flying, and they cast him out. He found his way eventually to a community of fliers like himself, all bent on raising flight to the level of art.

"Here were gulls who thought as he thought. For each of them, the most important thing in living was to reach out and touch perfection in that which they most loved to do. And that was to fly. They were magnificent birds, all of them, and they spent hour after hour each day practicing flight, testing advanced aeronautics."

Because he flew best, Jonathan was the teacher. "He spoke of simple things—that it is right for a gull to fly, that freedom is the nature of his being, that whatever stands against that freedom must be set aside, be it ritual or superstition or limitation in any form."

He concentrated on expanding his students' awareness of what flying was and what it could become. The possibilities were beyond most of their imaginations.

"Why is it," Jonathan said, "that the hardest thing in the world is to convince a bird that he is free, that he can prove it for himself if he'd just spend a little time practicing? Why should it be so hard?"

The running world has its Jonathan Livingston Seagulls—more of them all the time. And they're expanding consciousness of what the activity is and can be. They're pushing back the psychic limits of traditional running.

Running is natural, but runners aren't "normal" in an automated era. In the general community, they are odd birds to start with because they run. They find it necessary to explain why, over and over and over again. The community assumes a man who runs must be running *for* or *from* something, so runners have tended to phrase their answers in those terms.

"For most gulls," Richard Bach wrote, "it is not flying that matters, but eating." For most runners it is not running that matters, but the results gained. This has been the traditional way of looking at running. It has limited runners' vision to one or perhaps two dimensions.

Until a few years ago, running was competitive sport– period. A runner raced as long as he was racing well against other runners and the returns justified the investment. Then he stopped.

The fitness scare of the 1960s added a second dimension to running. Thousands of non-athletes and former athletes turned to running in hopes of saving their lives.

Both aims are worthwhile. Letting ambition run to its limits and reclaiming health and vigor are satisfying in themselves. But they leave a big open space in between for runners who see that fitness is just a beginning, and that big competition isn't everyone's ideal end.

The third dimension—the one between joggers and racers—begs for people to fill it. And they have. They are the Jonathan Livingston Seagulls of the running world. They've caught a fresh vision of what running can be, and they're chasing it. Above all, they like to run and therefore can lose only if they stop running.

This book is for those of you, those of *us,* who look at running as too good a thing to throw away, who have this vision of what running can be, and know if we run for fun we can run forever. This book is to help us keep the vision in focus.

A community of fun-runners is growing up which is showing that running is more than "flapping around from place to place." A... a... *car* does that!

THE ONLY WAY TO LOSE

The day started as they all had. At 6:03, my "alarm clock," a commuter train for San Francisco, rumbled past the window. I got up more from habit than desire, stumbling over the ironing board in the dark as I came back from the bathroom. The border of the sky over the mountains was just beginning to brighten as I shuffled out of the rocky driveway and headed east. Both feet hurt. They had for quite awhile. Sometimes it was one, sometimes the other. This time it happened to be both at once.

I ran through the empty parking lot of the new apartment house with the "No Trespassing" sign, and then over the bridge with "No Pedestrians" sign. No one was up this early to stop me. I went down almost to the *Runner's World* office, then came back on my regular bike commuting route through the high school grounds. The run took a half hour, about average for me since my feet went bad.

The only thing out of the ordinary about this run was my feeling that it would be my last—or at least the last for a long time. Surgery on the worst of the feet was scheduled for three hours later.

It had seemed so minor. One Saturday, I ran my customary two hours. The next morning, my left heel was sore. But of course that didn't stand in the way of a run. My feet were often sore after long runs. The pain would go away in a day or two.

This one didn't go away. At first I called it a bruise and refused to see that it was anything more serious than that. I treated it as I would a bruise: by ignoring it and running as always.

I raced 20 miles the following week, and 18 miles the week after that—and had other long races periodically for two more months. By then an ugly lump had grown on the heel that once was nearly smooth. It glowed red from irritation and inflammation inside. I was having to cut short my runs and to skip races. It was more than a bruise.

Finally I went to see a podiatrist. He said I had bursitis and that it often hits runners in their heels.

"Take a week off," he said. I took a week off and it didn't help any.

"Take two weeks off," he said. Again, there was no improvement.

"It looks like you're going to need six months off," he said.

That's when I looked for another doctor. More than eight months after the pain started, I found Steve Subotnick. He prescribed " conservative" treatment—inserts for my shoes—and said "keep running." This helped, but I had let the problem go too long. It wasn't getting any worse, but it wasn't getting much better, either. I could do short, very slow runs. But anything longer than 45 minutes or faster than eight-minute pace left me hobbling for weeks. This was no good.

"I'm ready for surgery," I volunteered to Dr. Subotnick. I brought up the subject. I couldn't see having this thing with me much longer. It had been just shy of a year already since the heel started hurting.

"It looks like that's the way we're going to have to go," he said.

"Okay, how soon?"

"How about Tuesday?"

My jaw dropped. I'd expected him to say something like the middle of next month.

"Well, uh, sure. I guess that's okay."

He warned me that I may be off my feet for a long time—a month at least, maybe months. I said I hadn't really been running in months, anyway, so what the hell.

"If it will cure me, I'm ready. Ready and eager."

"It will." Dr. Subotnick sounded so sure of it that I wasn't dreading the cutting. Not at first. But then he had to postpone it for several more days. I had those extra days to think and talk about the operation. Dread starting seeping into the hope, the same way it it does before big races, which have pain with their promise.

A month away from running. What's a month beside the 15 years I've already run, and at least that many more which should be ahead once I'm mended?

What a month is is the longest runless period I've had since 1958. And I get withdrawal symptoms after even a day away. Physically, I know I can bounce back quickly. But my addiction isn't purely physical.

Minor surgery. That's all it is. The doctor goes in and cuts away the excess bone that has grown in the heel. It's almost as simple as pulling a tooth.

But "minor" surgery is someone else's. If he's going to take a chunk out of my heel bone, that's major enough for me, thank you. And I don't walk and run on my teeth.

Dr. Subotnick said I was 99% sure of recovery from this—and that by hurting a lot now, temporarily, I could avoid hurting a little, permanently.

I had faith in the doctor's good judgment and firm hands. But even he couldn't control the 1% chance that this wouldn't work and that I'd be stuck for life with a defective foot. Feet don't come with replaceable parts.

The hope won out over the dread, and I decided the surgery was worth the small risk and inconvenience.

"Well, here it is."

The skinny, blue-eyed nurse with orange lipstick put her hand on my shoulder and held up a clear plastic pill bottle. I'd asked to see it. I wanted to see what I'd been carrying around in my left heel these many months.

I didn't expect to see anything so big. Floating in pink liquid were two rough-edged white chunks with stringy red threads hanging on them. Both were as big as the ends of my thumbs. Until a few minutes before, these had been parts of my heel, cutting into my tendon.

Dr. Subotnick didn't trust me. And with good reason.

"Normally," he said, "casts are optional in cases like this. But I know if I didn't put one on you, you'd be out trying to run in two days. You'd mess up all the good we've done you."

He slapped on some extra strips of plaster, "just to be sure you don't try anything funny. I have to do this with you runners. You're like hyper-active 13-year-old boys."

In the 20 days we were together, the cast and I never had more than an uneasy peace. The sudden loss of running brought on depression and irritability. It showed up in physical symptoms:

● Appetite down so low I lost as much as eight pounds, even without burning up much food.

● All-day drowsiness and listlessness that had me more tired than I am when I'm running.

● Waking up at 4 o'clock in the morning, twitching and not able to get back to sleep.

● Headaches and stomach aches.

I didn't feel guilty about missing running, as some runners do at times like this. And I wasn't worried about deteriorating condition. I knew it would come back right away. I'd just lost something

I'd come to crave. I'm addicted and I was going through withdrawal. I knew this is a fairly normal reaction.

I remembered writing about the Baekeland Study. An M.D., Frederick Baekeland, tested the effects of "exercise deprivation." The first thing he found was that it was hard to recruit subjects.

"It proved very hard," he said, "to find subjects who exercised regularly and yet were willing to deprive themselves of exercise for a month. Notwithstanding the fact that they were offered higher pay than usual, many prospective subjects (especially those who exercised daily) asserted that they would not stop exercising for any amount of money."

He settled for three-day-a-week athletes, who weren't so deeply addicted. Even they showed withdrawal symptoms.

While I was off, I read two stories in *Track & Field News* which touched on this same thing. Both were about 1968 Olympians who'd been through long layoffs after Mexico City.

Vince Matthews grew restless. "I had a lot of excess energy," he said, "but I was just sitting around the house. I would play basketball and handball in the parks, but it wasn't enough to burn up the energy I had." He started running again in 1971, and wound up with an Olympic championship a year later.

Tracy Smith injured an achilles tendon in 1969 and was out of heavy running for two years. He said he was "deeply depressed. I had been training three hours a day, and to go from that to nothing was terrible. I would wake up shaking, and the doctor said it was actually a physical withdrawal. I had so much mental and physical energy and nothing to use it up."

Tracy joined the Los Angeles Police Department "because I needed something demanding and exciting..." When he started running well again, he resigned from the force.

Knowing these things are normal made them no easier to handle when they were happening to me.

I'm no good at doing what's good for me. I tried a lot of substitutes for running, managing to get in some exercise almost every day that the cast was on. But I wasn't very loyal to it, and none of it was nearly enough to put down the withdrawal pangs.

A day after the operation, I crutched my way around the block —one of the longest, hardest and slowest "workouts" of my life. A week later, with the walking cast on, I hobbled a mile. It took a half-hour and produced bleeding toes. Another week after that, I was on a bike, pedalling not less than 10 miles a day with the cast still on. I tried to keep up my stretching exercises but they were harder to do when I wasn't running. I found excuses to skip them.

There was no life in any of these. I did them out of a feeling of obligation, and to keep me from going out of my bloody mind. These things weren't the same and they weren't enough. They were like an alcholic drinking coffee, or a junkie taking tranquilizers— mild, ineffective substitutes. Running is stronger medicine, and it fills a bigger need than exercise.

When three weeks had passed, I was thinking the leg was almost normal—and was feeling smug about my speedy recovery.

"Go ahead and take it off, Barbara," Dr. Subotnick told his nurse. He was busy in another room with another runner.

Barbara cursed under her breath at the thickness of the cast as the cutter repeatedly caught and jammed. Finally, she cut the undersock and ripped off the last stubborn piece of plaster—the inch-thick plate on the heel. She cut away the dressing. And there it was.

It looked awful. The calf hung limp like a dressed chicken. It was weak and flabby from no work. The skin on the lower leg was a deathly yellow, and was covered with stubble of shaved hair. The foot was dirty, and it had greenish-black bruises, oval-shaped and three or four inches long, down both sides and across the top.

The incision was caked with dried blood and 12 sutures poked out like legs of a centipede. It took a curved course from the ankle bone down to the bottom of the heelbone, on the outside of the foot. The area where the bump had been was red and swollen.

"Okay, jump down off the table," Dr. Subotnick said, motioning to the floor beside the examining table. The gleaming tile looked 40 feet away. I held tight to the edge of the table, and slowly lowered the good leg to the floor. Then the one that was the patient. I put weight on the toes. Felt okay. I loosened my grip on the table and let myself roll down toward the heel. "Aarrgh!"

I had no control. The foot seemed to go down eight inches further than it's supposed to. Electric-shock pains shot through the tendon. The nurse rolled a stool under me, and I plopped down heavily. I wasn't as healed as I thought.

How long would it take for the wound to heal completely, and for the strength and stretch to come back? Or would it come back?

"Maybe a few weeks, maybe months," Steve said. "It all depends on whether you want to get well or you want to keep soaking up sympathy."

An angry winter wind from off the Pacific coughed across the track, picking up puffs of light brown dust and chalk. Hurdles from last night's meet littered the straightaway, as if left by a hurricane. The track was empty except for four 10-year-old boys destroying the fallen hurdles. They stopped their game for a few minutes to laugh behind their hands and point at the funny man hobbling around the track.

The stitches had come out that morning, and I felt I was finally completely under my own power again. Nothing was holding me together. Even if I ran only five seconds, I'd know. I'd know where I was starting from.

I looked at my watch. "Maybe I'll make a minute."

I got to the first bend. "It hurts. But it's tolerable, and it isn't getting any worse. Maybe I'll go a 220."

At the 220, still feeling okay. "I'll go a lap."

The lap took almost five minutes. I walked another lap, faster than the running one.

Nothing had changed much since that morning six weeks earlier. The days had gotten enough longer that there was full daylight at six o'clock. I was already awake when the Southern Pacific 6:03 rumbled past the window.

I headed east. The new apartment house was finished now, and the parking lot that I used as a shortcut was full of cars. The "No Trespassing" sign was gone. The bridge over the expressway still still said "No Pedestrians," but no one paid any attention.

I turned around near the *Runner's World* office and came back home through the school grounds, seeing the same habitual runners there that I always saw. I seemed to feel better than I had before the operation. Not perfect, but better. But who remembers pain? I seemed to be ready to go back to thinking and talking about better things than my feet.

I had lost but now I was back. For the first time in 15 years, I had lost in the only way it was possible for me to lose—and that was not to be running at all. I wasn't running because I'd lost sight of the vision of what running is to me, and I'd lost touch with the voices from inside. I'd hurt myself.

This time I had recovered, but not before being convinced I never wanted to lose this way again.

REVIEWING L.S.D.

Remember that the boundaries of long slow distance were set down in 1969. They reflect the state of the art as it was then. It has changed. One problem with a book is that it can't reflect that change. It freezes ideas in time. It stops them and preserves them at the time they were first put on paper, like photos in a scrapbook.

Yet ideas don't stand still, any more than time and people do. The LSD idea has changed, evolved since *The Humane Way to Train* went down on paper in 1969. Times have changed. The six runners profiled in the book have changed. They've changed jobs and changed scenes. They've gone in and out of running and racing, in and out of shape while riding the tides of good and bad fortune.

The sport itself has changed. Long distance running and racing —above the normal track and cross-country limit of 10,000 meters —were only children in 1969. Since then, they've spurted through sometimes clumsy adolescent growth and are approaching maturity.

In 1969, there were fewer than 40 marathon races in the United States, and not more than a thousand active road racers. Five years later, there were almost five times that many marathons, dozens of times more road races both below and above 26 miles, and tens of thousands of runners (many of them non-racers) who saw the long distances as their special arena.

These runners have created an attitude of acceptance for all runners who use the streets, roads and parks, for whatever reason. They've created a bigger need for long slow distance running, and have changed the meaning of the words.

Long slow distance. How far is long? How fast is slow? How much is distance? Asking these things is like asking how high is up. There isn't any any one pat answer.

Now that so many more people are racing marathons, "long" isn't as far now as it was then. Eight to 15 miles is a typical day's work. It wasn't that way in 1969.

"Slow" is now closer to many runners' racing speeds, and it doesn't seem so slow any more. Six- or seven- or eight-minute miles is as fast as they ever need to go. Before marathoning grew up, they thought they had to go faster.

The inflation of training mileages has devalued "distance." More so than in 1969, "more-is-better" is a guiding principle, and not a healthy one. One-hundred-mile weeks are standard, 150 and up is the diet of champions, and 50 is judged barely adequate.

The whole concept of LSD is what it always was: a philosophy of comfortably-paced, enjoyable running. But the surroundings of it have changed. When LSD was proposed in 1969, it was a radical idea. It was a plea to cut down speed and add distance. Now, just a few years later, it sounds conservative since it often is a call for cutting down distance and adding speed.

The boundaries were drawn in 1969. They haven't changed. But since then there has been poking around inside and outside of them, clearing the ground, planting and harvesting several crops. The book contained seeds of growth and seeds of destruction, depending on who used it how. No idea is better than those who use and abuse it.

The first book set out the boundaries, which need no changing. There is a need to add to what is there, to explain and clarify and refine.

There is a need, now more than before, for some speed, some restraint, some flexibility—particularly among runners using LSD. It is too tempting for them to go slower and slower, longer and longer, counting miles instead of good experiences, or collecting racing times at the expense of good health.

The end to all of this mileage escalation and of overracing will be to arrive back where they started, with no running at all. After you've had it, not having it is worse than nothing. Too much of something leads to too much of nothing.

TOO MUCH OF SOMETHING

The *LSD* book features six runners, all of whom arrived at that way of running independently. They had thrived on it up to the time the book was written. They haven't stood still since then.

Time has been kindest to Jeff Kroot. Of the six, he has been most successful at keeping his head in the right place and his feet on the ground. Jeff moved to the country after the book came out. He worked at designing and building rustic houses, and he was content to run in the woods near his home without getting caught up in mile counting or speed traps. He rarely came out to race, but raced well when he did.

Jeff is a man of theories. And most of his theories make good sense. He told me during one of our hour-long phone talks:

"Van Aaken, Lydiard, Henderson, all of them. I've decided you can put them all in your pipe and smoke 'em. They're all doing the same thing. They're trying to make us think running is a technique sport, and that they've found the one right technique. But all of their fancy looking programs are what Lydiard himself calls 'just a lot of eyewash.'

"The only things a runner should be concerned with are (1) getting enough miles to be fit for what he wants to run, (2) keeping his energy reserves high, (3) avoiding injuries and (4) staying interested. As long as he's doing these things, it doesn't matter what kind of running he's doing. The 'best' way to run is the way that satisfies these needs."

Jeff stayed at a steady 40-60 miles a week, because to do more would have worked against the aim he outlined. He stayed healthy, fit for racing and eager.

Bob Deines ran the fastest 50-mile in US history in 1970, but was to become a victim of his own habits.

He said after the 50, "Basically, I try to be as lazy as possible in all things. That is my goal, in life and as it applies to running. The easiest way for me to get 100 miles per week is to run for two hours immediately upon getting out of bed. As I grow older and more serious in my efforts to achieve absolute laziness, I feel less of an attraction to most races, as there are few races which really attract me—except from the entertainment angle."

Deines didn't think of two hours of running each morning as work. But he did feel compelled to do it— to do it every day,

come what may. Even when he hurt himself, he kept doing it. Injuries grew more serious, races less frequent. Then runs grew shorter. He began having to skip some. Finally, he quit running altogeth-
er. He still hasn't started back up again. He's out of the habit.

Amby Burfoot graduated from school into teaching. He needed years to adjust his running to the new set of responsibilities and
the tighter time framework.

After starting teaching, he said, "I had so little training I was in
the worst shape I'd been since high school. Teaching has been much
more demanding than I could have imagined. It has been a real
struggle to go out and run after a tough day in the classroom."

Burfoot said when he ran "it seemed I had to run fast to save
precious minutes for planning, correcting papers, etc. Consequent-
ly, I ran quite hard, didn't enjoy it as much, and found rationaliza-
tions for skipping workouts. This 'fear of the precious minute' was
quite obviously neurotic, but this is the way I react in a societal position I don't relish. Now I'm struggling to get my training back on
an even, slow keel."

Amby adjusted. He quit struggling, ran less than he had in 1968
(when he'd won the Boston marathon) and is racing almost as fast
as then.

Ed Winrow was just starting college coaching when the LSD
book came out. Appearances to the contrary, coaching isn't the
ideal spot for a runner wanting to continue. The rules against coaches competing are generally ignored, and have been in Ed's case. But
there are other complications. Running is a rather selfish activity.
It has to be a "me-first" thing, and it takes time. Coaching is a giving activity. It is "them-first," and it takes even more time. There
is a conflict.

Ed resolved the conflict in the only way a good coach can...by
cutting down his own running to concentrate on teaching what he'd
learned.

"The runners responded slowly physically but fast mentally to
LSD," he said of his early coaching. "They learned to relax and enjoy running. They knew I didn't expect them to win all the time. I
kept telling them, 'We're not fast, but we're funny.'

"I've been patient with the team, and they have been very patient with me. If we can develop a spirit and enjoyment for running
and competition, the battle will be won. You wouldn't believe how
these young athletes associate pain, discomfort, etc., with being a
good athlete. They have the mistaken misconception that it (running) is all or nothing."

Tom Osler takes the view that all-out often leads to nothing. He says, "Fitness is a stage you pass through on the way to top racing form." Tom has remained an incredibly healthy individual because he generally has practiced what he publishes. He has written, "I have concluded that the marathon race is a definite form of self-abuse for one who trains as I do (60-80 miles slow a week). That is, to stand on the road and tell yourself you will run as fast as possible for 26 miles is a most unnatural endeavor, and one which the body was not designed to withstand.

"I do it, and will continue to do it, because I like it. However, I am aware that as the fatigue progresses I am likely to become injured and to lower my overall resistance in a most foolish way. Most marathoners think that racing does them good. It does not, and only serves to decondition rather than condition the body."

After writing this, Tom injured his heel—while racing. He wondered whether the writing might have jinxed him.

"After writing the article 'Beating Man's Best Friend,' in which I described how to control attacking dogs," he says, "I was overcome by a pack of three canines on my favorite course. The attacks continued daily, and I was finally forced to abandon my course. My next article, 'Avoiding All Injuries,' described how I remained injury-free for eight years. A few months later, I suffered a serious injury of my left heel."

Tom wasn't able to race for a year. During that time, he told *Runner's World*, "I have avoided mailing my manuscript 'Marital Harmony for the Runner.' You will shortly received my article 'How to Avoid Being Raped While Training.'"

Tom knows better than anyone, though, that his injury wasn't a coincidence. Nor were the ups and downs of the other runners. There are few accidents in running, and highs and lows are usually quite predictable when we know the codes for reading these things.

Runners get trapped in those dead-end situations when they can't see the way out. Ironically, the best way to pry the eyes open is to get in these scrapes. Only then do we learn the values of compromise, flexibility, slowing down and stopping now so we can keep going later.

The hard way may be the only way for a compulsive, habitual runner to learn. It's the only way anything has gotten through to me. Let me back up and tell how I got to the operating table...

The newspaper office was air-conditioned. But as I pushed through the revolving door and out onto the sidewalk, hot and wet

night air slapped me in the face like a steaming towel. It tasted too thick to breathe.

The time-temperature sign on the corner flashed "12:58." Then "98." Almost one o'clock in the morning and down only a few degrees from the day's high of 101. It had been this way for a week or so. This was the year's August hot spell.

I went home to bed but couldn't sleep. My room on the north had saved the day's best for me. I lay there as I had all week, outside the sheets with a window fan flowing across me, trying without luck to coax a cool breeze from the sticky air and to coax a bit of sleep from the night. Once the sun came up there'd be no more chance for sleeping. And it would be too hot to do much else.

The new day was as hot as the last one. By nine o'clock it was already 100 degrees. I dreaded my run that morning more than usual, and I always dreaded them some. To run was often unbearable, yet not to run was unthinkable.

Even when hot and hurting, I was driven by it. I raced myself every day. I'd made the mistake two years earlier of measuring and timing all my runs, and keeping records for every one. Then I'd try to break those records every time out. It started quite casually. But from month to month the records grew harder to break.

I worked harder at going faster. I worried that I couldn't. My legs started screaming in revolt over the abuse they were taking. All of this escalated until I couldn't bear it any longer. Something had to snap. It snapped this 100-degree day in August 1966.

I was on the red brick track at Drake University for a series of fast 2½-lap runs. Three were planned. Halfway through the first one, I wasl already laboring. I sucked desperately at the muggy air, trying to get in enough to fuel my legs that ached all the way up the backs. I was sweating so violently I could nearly hear it. I was dizzy.

Next thing I remember, I was sitting on the infield with my head between my knees. I'd sat there a long time before I could think straight. And then I sat there a long time in the freshly cut and watered grass, thinking...

The first thing I remember thinking was, "Do I really need this?" There was never any doubt that I needed running, even then. But I didn't need *that kind* of running?

I asked myself what I liked least about running. The anwer was the hurting, hurrying and worrying I was doing so much of just then. Did I need that? I knew I could hurt less by slowing down. And by slowing down there'd be less hurrying. And if I didn't feel I had to hurry there'd be less worrying.

What would happen? Maybe I'd race slower. So what? Did I have to beat anyone? No one cared if I beat anyone or no one. I decided the only one who could beat me was me, and I'd been doing a lot of beating that I could very well do without.

I decided my main interest was in going long—long in terms of single runs and long in terms of years of running. The way to do that was to pace myself for the long haul. At the rate I was going, I couldn't last long.

What I liked most about running, even then, was a long stretch of road in front of me, and being able to run it comfortably. I had scheduled this kind of run only on easy, relaxed days—maybe once every week or two, when I was too sore to do anything else. It never failed to pep me up. Why not every day?

I was 23 years old and had been running year-round for the past eight of those years. But it was as if I was seeing running, seeing where I was and where I was going, for the first time. For the first time in memory, I wasn't training to race and was running to run. It was a fresh kind of exploration.

Instead of running headlong into the barriers of time and pain after going through a dark corridor of distance, I was slowed down enough to look around and inside myself. I saw things that had always been there but I'd never taken time to notice.

I was to build a new career on what would come to be known as LSD and fun-running and the writing that sprang from them. They were to take on the trappings and burdens of a system. But that would be later. I didn't start with those ends in mind. I just wanted to make Iowa's August a bit more tolerable.

And it was. August heat didn't seem as oppressive as before, now that I wasn't fighting it. That fall, the best season in Iowa, never looked better now that I was running without tiring. Even when the snow came in November, I wasn't bothered as much now that I didn't have to hurry. Iowa showed subtle beauty that I'd never seen before. But I started thinking if this place looked this good, how much better California must be with its mountains and ocean and without Iowa's Augusts and Februarys.

The bigger reason I had to go there, weather and scenery aside, was the racing in California. Road racing. There were road races year-round, and I wanted those races.

It wasn't meant to happen this way. I hadn't planned to race faster by running slower. That seemed impossible. I wasn't thinking of racing at all when I made my slowdown. I hoped maybe to *run* in long events, but not to *race* them. There's a big difference.

I wanted to finish, just finish—not compete.

But as soon as I quit wanting to race, all my racing immediately got faster, even short things like the mile. As soon as I quit trying to make speed come, it came. When I lost my fear of failing, I no longer could fail. Because I wasn't working hard every day any more, I was fresh and relaxed and eager for those rare hard days at races, no matter what the result.

As it turned out later, I came to liking racing too well and the results were too good. As soon as I got the chance in California, I ran them too often and too fast, and ran into a new sort of trouble. I lost my respect for the effort and recovery races require. I started wanting to run them every week and had the chance to do so. This combination led to the new trouble.

The pace and the number of races crept up so gradually. I couldn't see what was happening. I couldn't see any connection between race frequency and injuries. In 1971 I raced on consecutive weeks (a) 15½ miles, (b) six miles, (c) 50 miles, and (d) five miles. In the last one, my achilles tendon snapped. It was the weakest link and it said "enough!" I didn't run normally again for four months. But I didn't learn.

I didn't learn from past mistakes, so I repeated them, with the effects compounding. It wasn't as if the final blow came without warning, like a car without lights running me down in the night. It was as if the car started honking and blinking its light a mile away and I wouldn't move from its path.

The pain in the heel started just after the achilles had recovered. I raced heavily on it until I couldn't race any more. Then ran by my schedule until I couldn't run any more. Then I got my operation and thought over what had happened. Only then did I learn how much is too much, how I got there and how to get out.

REDEFINING L.S.D.

The point of the LSD experience of the six runners in the earlier book is this: they started running that way on impulse, before there was a name for it. They got hurt after it had become a rigid system.

They didn't sit down and weigh the alternatives and then say, "Ah ha, this one looks best." They slowed down because their bodies told them to do it. Longer and slower was the natural change to make for runners who had run themselves down by going too short and fast. They changed because it seemed like the right thing to do just then. The rationale for it grew up later. The name came later, and the trouble.

The trouble told these runners they needed to turn around and go back to a day when they trusted their impulses. They needed to go back before set schedules had evolved, before LSD had taken a name and the rigidity of a system. They needed to go back to natural running.

LSD itself needs to be redefined as "natural running," a primitive kind of running which is systematized only to the extent needed to deal with certain artificial conditions modern man faces. Timed races aren't natural, but they satisfy cravings that have no better outlet. Running in shoes on hard roads isn't natural, but these surfaces are about the only ones left.

"Primitive man may very well have loped barefoot over the veldt in pursuit of his dinner," Desmond O'Neill has written, "but he did his loping on soft surfaces, with only occasional high-speed bursts. Certainly he rarely had to run long distances at a fast steady pace on hard roads. And therefore he never evolved the body necessary for that sort of activity. That leaves us, his descendants, ill-equipped for our own self-appointed tasks, which we perform without out even the reward of a meal."

Okay, so we're not made for much of our modern running. Should we then forget it? "Of course not," O'Neill says. "Regular training can inure the body to many of the stresses of this sort of activity." *Inure*, he says. The word means "protect." By living within nature's laws most of the time, a runner inures himself to the troubles that lurk outside. If he steps outside the laws too often, though, he *injures* himself.

Running is natural, but racing hard for more than a hundred

steps at a time is not. Since running is natural, it should flow along its natural course without undue interference from times and mile counts. Since racing is artificial, the amount, pace and frequency of it demand strict controls to keep it from polluting all of running.

The activity has in it the properties to be healthy or unhealthy, constructive or destructive, relaxing or tensing, satisfying or frustrating, pleasurable or painful. The way the balance tips depends almost entirely on the way running and racing are combined.

The laws are simple:

1. Everything living must keep going and growing. To stop is to stagnate and wither. But to go too fast is to stumble and fall. Let it flow at its own rate.

2. The right pace is one that feels comfortable, neither too fast nor too slow. If it feels good, it's good for you. If it hurts, it can't be helping much.

3. It isn't nice to fool Mother Nature. When her feelings are hurt, she turns and hurts you back.

The way out of this trouble is as simple as the laws you broke to get there:

If you want to quit hurting, quit hurting yourself. If you want to quit feeling bad, be good to yourself. Nature will thank you by letting you keep running.

The Limits

NATURE'S OWN WAY

Arthur Newton, one of the best ultra-marathoners of all-time, once wrote, "Just consider wild animals, which on the whole are certainly much healthier than the average modern man. They run plenty, but never at any time for all they are worth unless obliged by absolute fear. Even then it is only being scared stiff that will make them extend to their utmost."

Animals certainly do go fast, but only for short distances, stopping before they are exhausted. It apparently is unnatural for them to run for long in a state that human physiologists call "oxygen debt." The animals don't know the reasons why, but they know they don't like feeling exhausted. So the all-out sprints they take are short ones.

German Dr. Ernst van Aaken says the same is true for man. It isn't natural for him to go more than perhaps 100 meters at full-tilt. An Italian physiologist, Rudolfo Margaria agrees saying that lactic acid—one of the body's main fatigue products—begins building after about 15 seconds of anaerobic (oxygen debt) running. A human can cover about 100 meters in that time.

It isn't necessary to remember the formula or the big words of the scientists. It's enough to know that it isn't natural to run for a long time or very often when breathing is labored and when legs are heavy, stiff and sore. Primitive man wouldn't do that. Primitive man took gentle, loping runs, broken occasionally by short and sharp bursts and with walking or rest when he tired.

Running at its purest is identical to that of the wild animal and primitive man: running without tiring by combining long easy runs and only brief explosions of speed.

But while advocating natural running, it would be wrong to neglect one thing: the fact that modern runners are far removed now from their natural state. Man was built to run away from emergencies. A reserve of power is built into him for these emergencies, which are largely absent from modern living.

His racing is a kind of contrived, artificial emergency that satisfies a primitive and natural urge to take calculated risks. Racing is one of these risks.

A race isn't meant to be comfortable. It's meant as a test of the limits, as a primitive lesson in survival. It's said that the only time animals in the wilds will run all-out for extended distances is when they're starving or trying to escape a bigger animal that's starving. Wild animals are in one situation or the other quite often.

But man rarely has life-or-death chases any more. So he has to create them. Running distance races is one way. No animal appreciates living so much as one who has been to the edge of death. No human appreciates the comforts of civilized living so much as one who has faced a primitve challenge and has been most uncomfortable.

Dr. George Sheehan, the *Runner's World* medical editor, says that not to take risks, not to court dangers or to press some limits, is not to experience life fully.

"Every sport has certain risks," he says. "Consider mountain climbing, cycling, auto racing, the 'blood' sports. Our risks (in running) are certainly minimal. But they are there." Sheehan says it's becoming increasingly evident that "running is a relatively hazardous occupation, especially as so often happens with activities, in the very beginning."

Dr. Sheehan advises courting reasonable controlled risks like racing. He gets support from Dr. Sol Roy Rosenthall, professor of preventive medicine at the University of Illinois and an authority on risk-taking in sports. Rosenthal thinks risk-taking cravings came with the human mechanism.

"They were carefully calculated long ago," he says. "Risk became sport as well as necessity; natural risks evolved into challenges and physical feats. They helped mold man's codes of honor, pride and loyalty. They also prolonged his youth and prowess. In time, the old stimuli—the old dangers—were forgotten, but not the effects, not the way man felt. He is still happiest when physically threatened."

But the doctor adds, "Let's be sure we understand each other. I'm not advocating recklessness. There was nothing foolhardy about the risks your ancestors took. They were calculated risks, well calculated."

It helps to know how to calculate.

THE RUNNING ANIMAL

"Here is a theory," writes runner Philip Milner. "A person ought to run a lot, but he should seldom run as fast or as hard as he is capable of doing. Look not to charts for a way to treat the body. Look instead to dogs and cats and horses. They run much of the time from place to place. But unless a dog is trying to catch a cat, or unless a horse has a person sitting on its back hitting it with a stick, they seldom run as fast as they can."

Running moderately builds, running to the limits of endurance destroys, Milner says. The proof of this is not found in books but in watching people and animals and seeing how they react to stress.

"My theory has nothing going for it but its rightness," he says. "Subscribe to it and you win the respect of nobody else. Jogging moderately won't win the respect of the serious runners who will think you are frivolous. Nor will it convert the armchair cynics who will still think you are mad. But the jeering of the rabble is a small price to pay for the certain knowledge that your jogging has the sanction of dogs and horses and other sources of untraditional wisdom."

The various dogs I've grown up with have taught me more about how to run than have the various books I've read. One of the dogs, Liesel, was more of a runner than the others. Liesel was running in her blood. She was half greyhound and to run was her birthright.

From the day I rescued the three-month-old pup from oblivion at the hands of a veterinarian, she ran with me. She struggled at first. Her little legs couldn't keep her up with me. By the end of slow one-hour runs, the fuzzy pup would be puffling along 200 yards behind, but sticking with it, uh, doggedly.

She grew up fast. Before long, it was I puffing along 200 yards behind her. She carried enough speed and endurance in reserve to sprint ahead and off to the sides to explore, to chase squirrels and to terrorize smaller dogs. Unaware that she'd wandered into their paths, she'd stand and give drivers "what's-wrong" looks as they screeched to a stop inches from her.

For her safety and my serenity, I had to start chaining Liesel up while I ran. She couldn't understand why. She tried to slink away whenever she saw me grab the chain. She'd sulk when I slipped it around her neck. And she'd whine as I disappeared down the driveway.

But the other 23 hours a day she was free to roam at will on an eight-acre farm. There were friends to run with, horses to chase, and best of all there weren't any visible boundaries restricting her. Except during that miserable hour a day when I ran and she couldn't, Liesel was a calm, happy dog leading a good life.

Then her world was turned upside down. She went to live within the 20- x 30-foot fence of a back yard in suburbia. The only time she got out was when I took pity and let her run with me.

Being cooped up like this, she turned steadily neurotic. She slouched around morosely most of the day, she barked at shadows and cowered fearfully in corners. Once she preferred the outdoors. Now she tried desperately to get inside to hide. Once in, she wouldn't leave unless dragged out.

But when I let her out to run, she'd be her old self again. Her super-self. She'd almost knock me and the door down on the way out. It was as if in five minutes she was trying to wipe away the days of captivity. She leaped, sprinted and frolicked with unrestricted joy, going in no particular direction but acting elated simply to be going again.

After a mile she settled down, content to trot along with me. Her neuroses were temporarily put to rest by the run. When we got home, I didn't have to lay a hand on her to get her out of the house. She left confidently. For one hour of the day, she had tasted freedom, and she was happy until the next day. Her master had, and still has, the same basic need and felt the same way.

It's a winter morning, still dark and the rain and hail are beating on my head and shoulders. There's only a T-shirt and shorts between me and the elements as I splash down deserted main street.

I pass the pet store window. A squirrel monkey gives me a quizzical stare with his big black eyes. It's as if he's thinking, "I'm glad I'm not human. I'm warm, cozy and well-fed. Imagine being out in the rain and cold with hardly any clothes on at this time of the day. Humans are strange."

Drivers on their way to early jobs give me startled looks as they notice me along the sidewalk. They turn to their passengers and say, "Crazy! Why would anyone be out running on a day like this—or any day—when he could get where he's going easier and faster by driving!"

A little farther along, I pass a house with a man standing behind his picture window. He glances at me and shakes his head as if to say, "I'm glad I'm not a runner. I'm here in my warm house, comfortable and filled with a good breakfast. Look at him."

Monkey, driver and homeowner all have the idea I'm the one who's having problems. That I'm the slave of a running schedule. Trapped in it. But I'm not in a cage. And a cage by any other name —store window, car or house—is still a cage that cuts down freedom of movement. We spend most of our lives in one kind of cage or another. For an hour a day, I have to break out, I *get* to break out. A guy can take only so much warmth, coziness, convenience and good food.

Running satisfies needs far deeper and more basic than showing me I can run a three-hour marathon or keeping my weight below college level or tuning up my plumbing. In a dozen or more ways, running serves as a vital counter-balance to the often oppressive weight of modern living. Everyone needs to restore a balance.

● The more noisy and crowded life becomes, the more we need a quiet time alone with our thoughts.

● The more rushed the pace of living, the more we need to slow down and live.

● The easier and more comfortable our daily existence, the more passive, the more we need activity, effort, even a bit of pain.

● The more secure we become, the more we need to take occasional risks.

● The more we're forced to live and work indoors, the more we need to escape to the outdoors.

● The more we're burdened with mental work, the more we need to strike a physical balance.

● The more complex our life-style, the more we need a simple, uncluttered routine.

● The higher the level of boredom, the more we need excitement.

● The more anonymous and lonely we feel, the more we need attention and companionship.

● The more we're alienated from one activity, the more we need strong attachment to another.

● The more we meet with collective repression, the more we need individual expression.

● The more we're swamped with mass-produced things and thinking, the more we need personal creations.

● And the more we become civilized, the more opportunities we need to revert briefly to our primitive state.

This last point ties all the rest together. Man's mental capacity has evolved at a runaway pace. His body and instincts haven't kept up. While man's mind has created a high-speed, mechanized, industrialized, computerized, urban culture, he's physically and emotionally not unlike his tribal ancestors who roamed and hunted the open spaces a hundred centuries ago.

Throwing man into the strange new environment has confused him. He has surrendered his most basic activities in the name of ease and comfort. And is paying a high price for it, as surely as my dog who was cooped up in a back yard of suburbia.

Man is cast into an environment that's alternately unstimulating and overstimulating. He bounces wildly from a sterile existence with no meaningful acitivity to a frantic one with too much activity to absorb. This throws him off-balance and creates a need to return to the basics. To use his own mind and body as an artistic tool. To work for and with his small tribal group. And to be in and live in delicate harmony with himself and natural habitat.

Running—because it's individual, is somewhat creative, because there's often a tribal relationship among runners, and because the runner is closely allied with nature—satisfies these innate needs. As "progress" continues its wicked pace, the need to fall back on animal instincts and run from it becomes more urgent.

I hope we can run well enough.

SIGNS AND SIGNALS

For running to fill animal needs, it has to last. It can't be stored away today and used another day. It has to keep coming. Injuries, both physical and psychic, are the roadblock to long-lasting running. And running injuries don't happen by accident.

Football players and Indianapolis drivers get themselves mangled accidentally, suddenly and decisively in their sports. Wham! Bang! It's all over. Runners don't have that kind of trauma, not unless it comes from forces outside the sport—like drivers of family cars on residential streets who think they're at Indy.

There are few accidents in running. But that isn't to say there are not a lot of ailments. Accidental injuries strike like hit-and-run drivers. In those cases, fate is at the wheel. There's not much we can do to stop them if we can't see them coming.

Almost none of these accidents happen to runners. Almost all of our injuries spring from overstressing. And since stress loads are controllable, stress injuries are almost 100% preventable. Controlling loads involves reading and heeding our own subtle signs.

This isn't easy. Our injuries would be easier to handle if the signs weren't so subtle. Earthquakes are easier to deal with than erosion is. Quakes weaken structures immediately while strengthening the will to rebuild. Erosion quietly wears away both substance and spirit. Little pains eat away drop by drop at both fitness and enthusiasm. Minor irritants, left uncorrected, grow into major troubles.

If a runner broke his leg tomorrow, he'd come back a few months later. He'd swear to do that every day he was away. But nagging pains, the kind that don't appear worthy of attention because they don't stop his running, gnaw at his resolve as they grow. By the time he realizes something is wrong, he may have lost his will to fight it. Running has lost its magic. His whole system feels out of tune.

The human body is a symphony of signs and signals. When all the instruments inside are playing together and are really getting it on, they make beautiful music. The head is the conductor. It chooses the music. The legs are the melody. The arms are the counter-balancing harmony. The heart and lungs beat out the rhythm. A thousand instruments contribute to the balanced whole. When they're in tune, the fragments blend into one.

But when one instrument hits a sour note, the whole orchestra's sound is off. It makes noise instead of music. When one is sour, the entire orchestra sounds out of tune. The time to correct the tuning is before the sour sound becomes too obvious. It takes a sensitive ear to hear it.

A runner goes out of tune either when he doesn't run enough or when he runs too much. When he doesn't run regularly, he grows sloppy. When he runs too much and too fast, he gets hurt. Either way, there are clear signals that something is wrong. Trouble comes not so much from being wrong, but from ignoring the early signals.

Nature isn't an ogre. She's really quite cooperative. When there's too much stress put on her, she doesn't lose her temper and release stress injuries and illnesses full-force. Instead, she patiently holds up gentle signs to remind us that things aren't quite right. The most common are:

1. Low-level and persistent soreness and stiffness in muscles, joints and tendons.

2. Frequent mild colds, sore throats and headaches.

3. Swelling of the lymph glands, particularly under the arms.

4. Skin eruptions (acne, cold sores, etc.).

5. Excessive nervousness, depression and irritability.

6. Nagging fatigue and sluggishness that lingers from day to day.

7. Aching stomach, often accompanied by appetite loss.

8. Diarrhea or constipation.

9. Unexplained drops in performance.

10. Disinterest in normally exciting activities.

It's best to take note of these reminders, and to take appropriate corrective action (which normally means lowering the stress load). Reminders get progressively less gentle. Monitoring the signs and signals is a kind of proof-reading of yourself. Proof-reading of a book or magazine involves stopping screwups at the source, before they get into print. The better proof-reading an editor does, the less it's noticed. He may catch 99 of a hundred but the one that slips through to the readers is the one that makes him a bad proof-reader. Once the errors go public, they're easy to see but hard as hell to correct.

Running has the same sort of thing working. Preventive medicine might be called "proof-running." That means catching injuries and illnesses before they happen. Proof-running requires a close reading of your own signs and reactions. It's a quiet job and, like proof-reading, is going best when it's noticed least. Physical break-downs, once they happen, are easy to see and diagnose but hard as hell to treat. They're best avoided when they're caught early, and they're best caught by tuning in to pains and reading them for what they are.

Occasional mild pain is at least a worthwhile companion, if not a good friend in disguise. Pain is an innocent messenger. But runners tend to treat it in the way ancient kings did. Their messengers ran from one outpost to another, carrying news. They didn't make the news. They just relayed it. If the news was good, the king rewarded the bearer. But if the news was bad, the messenger was killed—as if he were responsible.

That's the way we treat the messages of the body. When they sing out good feelings, we reward them. But when they cry out in pain, we try to kill that pain—either by suppressing it artificially, or by ignoring it, thinking that by pretending it isn't there it won't be.

Pain isn't the culprit, though, any more than the king's messenger was. Pain doesn't make the news. It only delivers it. Pain only carries the message that something has gone wrong out in the provinces, and that it's time to dispatch a rescue team to get to the source of the trouble. Killing the symptoms while ignoring the causes never won anyone any battles.

But avoiding all pain and stress never won anyone anything, either. A man who never stretches himself to the point of pain never increases his ability to stretch. The yogis have been saying this for thousands of years. The guiding principle of yoga is "stretch without straining and you'll improve flexibility; strain and you'll snap." The yogi says stretch to the edge of tolerable pain, then back off a bit and hold that position. A runner can live by the same law, pushing himself only to the point where running starts to hurt, then backing off to hold a more comfortable pace.

"The goal," says Dr. Hans Selye, author of the stress theory, "is not to avoid stress. Stress is part of life. It is a natural by-product of all-out activities. There is no more justification for avoiding stress than for shunning food, exercise or love. But in order to express yourself fully, you must first find your optimum stress level... It is not easy. It takes almost constant self-analysis."

3

The Run

THE BALANCE

The same pattern applies to anyone who wants to run this way. Ten-mile-a-week fun and fitness runner or 100-mile-a-week marathoner, the general advice is the same.

1. There are but two speeds—gentle and all-out. All-out running is tiring. It can't be done very often or for very long. Unless all-out efforts are rationed, they tear a person apart.

Gentle running gives the feeling that it can go on forever, a run-without-tiring feeling. It can be done as often and as long as good sense and enthusiasm allow. Gentle running builds.

Both kinds of running, gentle and hard, have their values when kept in balanced proportions—at least 10 gentle parts to every all-out one.

2. The running pace is either gentle or hard, but not perfectly even within those extremes. It changes as intuition dictates, not according to the hands on a stopwatch or the numbers on a pace schedule. "Gentle" doesn't always mean the slowest possible. "All-out" doesn't have to mean the fastest ever.

3. There are three distances—short, average and long. They're all based on the average of all the days' runs over the weeks and months. The average sets the boundaries.

Short runs are for rest and recovery. They're about half the daily average.

Long runs consolidate the gains of the week and give an extra shot of endurance. They're about twice the daily average, never more than three times.

Races, those rare all-out runs, aren't more than two or three times normal, either. Build the ability to go longer from the middle and bottom, not from the top.

4. The running can be measured either by time or distance— but not both at once. Combining known time with known distance creates the urge to break records, which runs counter-to the purpose of gentle effort.

Of the two, running by time is more convenient than running by distance. With time, there's no need to measure courses or to stay on set routes, and there's no urge to hurry through a run. An hour can't be rushed. Eight miles can.

5. The running is consistent, but each day is not the same as every other. The weeks' running flows in waves, from long to short to average to short to long again, highs and lows following each other in natural sequence.

6. There is a proper setting for each of the types of running. Short gentle runs are like vacations or days off and require soothing surroundings—forest trails, parks, beaches.

Average runs are the workday runs. They are the biggest part of the formula. They're done close to home, when and where they're most convenient and fit into the daily routine with the least fuss. The easier they are to fit in, the more likely you are to keep doing them.

Long runs are special. They are the on-foot equivalent of a long weekend drive in the country. They deserve a countryside course.

7. The running can and should satisfy three psychic needs— the need to be along and to look around and to clear the mind of cluttering thoughts, the need to be with like-thinking people and to talk with them, and the need to wrestle with yourself to see what's inside.

Solo runs, short and average distances, do the first.

Social runs make long distances pass quickest and easiest, and satisfy the second need.

Speed runs, hard races, take care of the third.

Keep the elements in proper balance, and they do the same for you.

SOLO RUNNING

I stand at the front gate, winding my wristwatch longer than it needs to be wound. I'm waiting for the sharp, clean, after-the-rain air and the first light of the winter morning to chase the sleep from my head.

The paper boy wheels into the driveway and slides sideways to stop. He sees me and is startled for a second. Then he cocks his head and sizes me up. A grown man in his sorts and T-shirt in the early-morning cold. In most towns, a paper boy wouldn't know what to make of this sight, at this or any other time of day. This boy sees this all the time.

"You going jogging?" he says, his warm words turning white as they meet the cold air. I tell him yes, that I'm going for a *run*— emphasizing that last word to distinguish it from jog.

"I can't see much fun in jogging myself," the boys says. "But lots of people around here seem to do it. Here's your paper."

It's a few minutes past six in the morning when I leave home. I see another runner before I've gone a block. I'll see 10 more before I finish, or on a freshly-washed day like today as many as twice that number.

Los Altos, the town where I live, is a running town. Its high school has a history of good running teams, having won something like 150 straight dual meets in track. The school from this town of 25,000 won the state championship a couple of years back.

The school kids start running the roads early. I remember seeing one of them out morning and night when he was 12 years old and five feet tall. I still see him. He's 16 now and more than a foot taller. And he's one of the top runners on that team which wins all the meets.

Older people run here, too. This is a suburb of commuters— of lawyers and doctors, engineers and business executives who are comfortably off. These are the graduates of the best school who are headed for the upper class. These are the kinds of people who want to hold onto their high stake in society. So a lot of them run to to stay fit.

Any time day or night the track at the high school has grown-up runners circling it. Others are on the streets. Los Altos is a good place to be a runner. Runners are accepted here because we're such a common sight. Los Altos is a running town, and by all appearances, I'm the slowest runner in it.

I'm known only for my persistence and my eccentricities. No one knows me for the work I do the rest of the day. No one knows that I have raced 500 times and still do race once in a while, or that I haven't stopped in a decade and a half. No one knows that I'm going five or more times as far as they might be, or that my effort at this pace might be 60% compared to their 90%. No one knows that on the seventh day, my runs stretch out to 15 miles or more. I don't care that anyone knows.

Because none of this is known or seen, it doesn't exist. All this is apparent in a short, slow glimpse of my run in Los Altos on weekday mornings. During those times, I'm a target... No, I think "target" is too strong a word. "Bait" might be a better one. Since I'm out on the streets of Los Altos every morning at the same time, in plain view, I'm attractive bait for other runners. Those who know me think I want company, and they try to run along with me. Those who don't know me think I should compete with them, and they try to set my pace for me.

It's fine that so many people are running now. After being alone on these streets for so many years, I'm glad to see others using them—as long as they keep their distance from me. Six days a week, I still like to be alone in the sense that no one is matching my strides or injecting their thoughts into mine. Six days a week, I have to be by myself this first half-hour to hour that I'm awake. It's the only time of my waking day that I'm alone. I need this to keep in touch with where and who I am. I don't need attention or company.

The front gate opens with a squeak. I haven't wanted to oil it because the squeak is my signal that a runner is here. The dog hears the squeak and barks a couple of times to wake me up. I hush her up and lie as quietly as I can for as long as it takes my friend to get cold or get bored and leave. The squeaking gate is the signal that he's gone, and that I can get up.

Later, when I see him again, I fake innocence. "Oh, I didn't hear you come. Guess I overslept this morning." I lie.

He says, "That's okay. I'll be over Thursday. Is 6:15 okay?"

"Uh, yeah. See you then."

On Thursday, I make a point of getting up and out before six. When I get back, his car is in the driveway. He comes back and says, "Guess I got here too late."

I say, "No, I started early. Couldn't sleep. Have to get to work early today."

He stays and reads the paper to me as I sigh and try to ignore him as I write. Finally he gets up to leave, saying, " See you Tuesday." He won't take the hint.

Today I'm alone. The "Shake Thy Friend" game is won. But there's still one thing standing between me and a good peaceful run with myself. That's another kind of game called "Race Thy Neighbor." I don't like to play. But some days I have no choice. It's always the nicest days like this one, when every would-be runner in town summons the ambition to throw back the covers early. Everyone who has graduated from *Aerobics* and can go two miles without stopping sees himself as a racer. He races the clock around his course, or better yet races a moving object.

I'm that kind of bait– slow-moving enough to be attractive. I don't time myself, but just take my time. I doubt that I ever move faster than eight-minute mile pace. I can move faster. I just don't want to on mornings like this.

I try to stay away from racers. If I watch for them, they're easy enough to avoid. They wheeze and stomp the ground like stampeding steers. I don't have to see them. I can hear them. And simply crossing the street or making a quick turn will end the chase. That's because the racer won't go off the course he has set for himself.

I won't do any chasing. But some days, like today, I'm provoked into racing back.

The neighbor-racing game is made up of subtle moves—like a chess match, not a street fight. You play by the unwritten rules. You never, never change directions to initiate a race, for instance. When two runners meet going different ways, they always smile and wave to each other. They aren't threatened when they know the other won't turn on them. That's too obvious and aggressive a move.

Races come only when neighbors meet by chance. When they meet heading the same way, they try to look like they're ignoring each other. You wouldn't run up beside another runner, tap him on the shoulder, look him square in the eye and say, "Let's see what you have inside." This just isn't done.

Instead, the aggressor and victim look straight ahead down the road. They size each other up only from the corners of their eyes. They run on opposite sides of the street so as not to make it look like a direct confrontation.

The trick is in drawing accurate first impressions of the potential opponent. How fast he's going. How lean he looks. How he's dressed. How he's running—gliding or straining? If appearances say you're overmatched, let the guy go. Races don't do anything for anyone unless they're fairly even.

You have to know, too, that you don't start racing with a burst of speed. You jack up the pace by degrees until it's too hot for one or the other. A burst would end the race quickly, decisively. Accelerating draws it out over blocks, sometimes miles.

No one ever slows down while the other runner can see him. That would be a surrender, an admission of defeat and loss of face. No, instead you turn off at a side street and pull into a driveway as if you're home.

Usually I wouldn't get involved in this kind of thing. I don't have time to race in the morning, and wouldn't risk doing it as a regular thing even if I had the time. But this isn't a usual day. Something about the air has brought out the runners and has brought out the racer in them.

I don't know the guys' names. So I call them by the streets they use. Covington looks disgusted when I won't take his bait. He has spent five blocks of his course catching up to me, and then I let him go right on past. I get a slight itch to race him, but get rid of it by saying, "A big man like him—he must weigh 180—can't last for long at that pace. He'll be home, showered and fed before I'm done running." Covington looks like an ex-football player who has kept his shape. He is proud of his legs and never covers them with long pants.

Campbell, on the other hand, dresses as if he's modeling for *Joggers' Wear Daily*. The easiest way to spot a beginner is by what he wears. He'll have on a slim-fitting $40 stretch suit, the kind of Adidas that no runner going more than a mile could stand, a towel wrapped around his neck and tucked in his jacket in front. Campbell prances past me with his head thrown back, striding the way he thinks runners should stride but don't. I let him go without an argument, too, but am more annoyed by this challenge than the first.

I take out my irritation on Summerhill. For all I know, Summerhill is innocent. He doesn't appear to have any ability at racing, or any intention to try it. He's wearing low-cut, one-pound basketball shoes and baggy work pants. Not the kind of outfit a man wears for racing—and certainly not for challenging a runner in eight-ounce nylon flats and nylon underwear.

The man may not want to race. But the German Shepherd on the leash in his hand gives him no choice. Big dogs have an attraction to bare, moving (even barely moving) legs.

Summerhill and his dog pull alongside, though on the other side of the street. The man doesn't look at me. I don't look at him. The dog doesn't look at either of us.

I accelerate, stretching out little by little. Enough to keep my competitors pressing but not so much that a gap opens up and they lose interest right away. It goes on like this for a block, two blocks, then three. By now, my pace feels faster than I should be going at this time of morning.

I see a stoplight and cross-street ahead and plan to turn there, hoping Summerhill and dog don't do the same. They're thinking the same thing. I look back and they're gone. They've turned a block earlier.

I ease off, wheezing back down to a more sensible pace. I'm tired and my knee hurts from the effort. I don't feel like I've won anything. There's nothing to win by racing on the streets of Los Altos at this time of day.

The runners on the streets of Los Altos have seen less of me in recent months, since I've started seeking out the quiet and soft places of town several days a week. Several days a week, I've run in school yards and parks. I've done it partly to avoid confrontations with street racers and friends alike, but mostly to get back down to earth after a long time away.

Not so long ago, I ran a race on grass and dirt. It wasn't much of a race as these things go. It was six laps around a school ground. There were only eight of us running. The significant thing about this race is that it was the first one in six or seven years that I'd run on purely "natural" surfaces—no concrete, no asphalt, no Tartan.

It had nothing but soft, rough grass and dirt. That surface hurt my time, of course. But the rush to faster surfaces has been hurting me and other runners in worse ways over the years, as we've lost touch with the ground.

Back in the late 1950s and early '60s, when I was growing up and learning to run, I thought I was underprivileged compared to the city boys. I lived in a small town in Iowa, a really small town of about 300. It was so small it had no paved streets and few concrete sidewalks. One main road running east and west was crumbling asphalt—we called it "oil"—but it was too narrow to run safely.

When I ran, I did it on the soft dirt and gravel roads of the countryside, or on the grass oval lined out around the football field. The school didn't have a real track.

When I ran on the roads, I wore heavy, low-cut tennis sneakers I'd bought for $2.98. The canvas had rotted and tape held the shoes together. When I ran on grass, I went barefoot. The only time I got to a real track and wore spikes was to race. The tracks of southwest Iowa were loose and slow in the spring.

I didn't have a coach giving out jazzy speed workouts. He was happy to see someone wanting to run at all, and was content to let well enough alone. He let me run what I wanted. The only injury I had in four years came when I tried to sprint a quarter-mile on the ice in mid-winter. I wasn't what you'd call smart then, but I was healthy.

It was no coincidence that I started breaking down the day I moved to the city to start to college, and I've been more or less broken down ever since.

When I got to Des Moines, I did almost all my running on the streets and sidewalks, or on the track in the stadium. There wasn't much choice. The only patch of grass was at the city golf course, and that was a five-mile run away on the streets and sidewalks. In those days, the five miles alone were more than a day's work.

The school furnished me with the best imported shoes. The coach gave me the best imported speed workouts. But I didn't improve much—a few seconds in the mile was all. I was too busy getting hurt and recovering from sore legs to get any kind of momentum going. I was never again to enjoy the alive, healthy snap I'd had in my legs in high school before asphalt and concrete became so much a part of my environment.

It's that way for almost everyone now as grass and dirt, even the old cinder and clay tracks, have given way to asphalt and concrete. It's partly our fault. We've made no real attempt to run away from the hardening of the earth. In the name of speed and convenience, we've run to the road.

Arthur Lydiard, the running prophet of the 1960s, preached roads and we listened. I listened to him as early as my last year of high school. But my roads then were still soft. They've gotten harder over the years.

Lydiard said, "You run on the roads for a specific reason. You run on the roads because you get good friction or traction. When you get good friction or traction, you can run more economically. You are using less muscles, and you're only using the muscles actually needed to drive you forward. This is what you want in running. Because you can run economically, you can run farther and faster aerobically."

So runners started using the roads more and more. And they started getting things like the bumps of bursitis on their heels. This happened, Lydiard said, because they didn't have good enough shoes. Harder surfaces required better-made, sturdier, heavier shoes. The design and fit were more critical than before. But he forgot, as we all have in our rush, that man's feet were no more designed to wear shoes—even the good ones Lydiard designed, than they were to run on smooth and unyielding roads.

My podiatrist, Steve Subotnick, says, "The human foot wasn't made to run over perfectly even, hard surfaces. It was made to roll and twist, to compensate for changing terrain, not to run in an every-step-the-same pattern."

For its health, the foot needs the roughness and "give" of grass, dirt and sand. Even hard dirt is better than hard asphalt. Shoes, no matter how good they are, can't compensate completely for the hardness and smoothness.

Dr. George Sheehan, the *Runner's World* medical columnist, thinks, "The worst thing that ever happened to feet was shoes—or perhaps the second worst after concrete. The two products of urban civilization have finally conquered the human foot, which in its primitive state, crossed continents, pursued wild game and danced for days on end."

But what can we do except make the best of a bad situation? We're so surrounded by hard roads and tracks that there aren't any other places a runner can go. We're so dependent on shoes, and our feet have gone so fragile from wearing them, that we couldn't do much barefoot running even if there were good places left to do it.

Making the best of the bad situation means getting off the hard roads some of the time and getting at least one step closer to the earth than usual. After being two steps removed—by paving and shoes—for so long, I'm seeing how important this is for not only my feet and legs but for my head too.

Getting off the roads once in a while is soothing and restful. That alone is a good enough reason to do it. Even if it were proven to me that there's no difference to the feet and legs between the hard and the soft, I'd still choose the soft when I could because my head likes it.

Anyone with an ounce of aesthetic sensitivity would have to feel the same. The hard places are the ones where machines and noise and smelly air live. The soft places are the home of growing, quiet and fragrant things.

I still do and probably will always run on roads on my "long" days. But the shorter, easier runs—as many as four a week—are now on any piece of uncovered ground I can find with room to take laps of more than a few minutes each. These places are neighborhood parks, school playgrounds, even road shoulders and dirt tracks as last resorts.

Across the street is a vast expanse of green grass, miles of it. But it's on the wrong side of an eight-foot barbed-wire-topped fence, marked "Los Altos Golf and Country Club—No Trespassing."

RUNNING GENTLY

How fast is slow? How hard is gentle?

Formulas are available that try to answer that. Seven minutes a mile was Arthur Lydiard's magic number. One booklet, *New Views of Speed Training*, talked about 80% of maximum speed for a given distance. Someplace else there was mention of running a minute per mile slower than one's fastest time at a distance.

The best answer, though, isn't to be found on a stopwatch. It's in the runner's heart. The best pacer for gentle runs is pulse. Running pulse rate is the runner's most sensitive and personal barometer of effort. The worst pacer is the wristwatch. It either holds the runner back or, more likely, stretches him too far. Either way, time sets a false standard for the run.

Pace is too important and delicate and varying a thing to be left to an unfeeling watch. The best pace is one where the style is fluid, the breathing is easy, the miles come comfortably, yet there's a feeling of controlled power in the running.

The watch has no way of knowing what this pace should be. It changes not only day to day but minute to minute. The pace of a single run may vary from six to nine minutes a mile, and yet be comfortable and controlled all the way.

How do you know this pace is right? You feel that it is, and you trust your feelings. And to verify that your feelings are correct, you check your pulse from time to time just after finishing. The figure you get is nothing like the resting figure, which gets an undue amount of attention among runners. The resting rate only reflects long-term results of running. It tends to drop as runners get in shape, though this isn't always true. Fit endurance runners often have resting heart rates in the 40s, and sometimes even in the 30s, but equally good runners may have pulses that race along in the 60s and 70s. Exercising rates, however, are more stable from individual to individual and offer immediate feedback on running's effects.

Listen to your heart. It's the best pacer you have. A runner can't get any training effect without pushing his heart rate well above resting levels. That's obvious. It's equally apparent that he can't go very long at his maximum pulse without collapsing. He has to find an optimum working percentage somewhere in between the two extremes.

Monitor the heart rate. It's your best indicator of effort. Running to your own best beat and knowing what it means are long steps toward staying fit and healthy.

Spot checks are sufficient. The simplest way to take pulse is to count the beat for six seconds and add a zero to the total. If the six-second count is 15, pulse is about 150. This isn't an exact system, but you don't need an exact figure.

Before too long, it's possible to "feel" pusle without stopping to take it. It relates closely to breathing and effort, and you get to know which rates go with which signs without having to count. One experienced "gentle" runner says, "If I make no effort to control my pace and only tune in to my body signs, I invariably come out with a 130 pulse at the end of my runs."

Dr. Ernst van Aaken says pulse rates during everyday runs should be about 130. According to van Aaken, "at a pulse frequency of approximately 130, the organism absorbs a maximum quantity of oxygen at a minimum breathing volume." He quotes a study by Bruno Balke, a noted exercise physiologist working in the US, to support his claim. Balke says the fatigue produced lactic acid only begins accumulating beyond a pulse rate of 120-130. Lactic acid is produced when runners are operating breathlessly.

Van Aaken points out that while this 120-130 level is fairly constant from person to person, fitter runners can go much faster than unfit ones while the heart is loafing along at this rate. One runner might go six minutes a mile with a 130 heart, while another may only go nine minutes. Time doesn't matter.

Instead of looking at pulse rate per se, however, it may be better to talk in terms of *percentages of maximum.* Maximum heart rates drop steadily with age. A 130 heart rate for a 25-year-old would be a much lower percentage than for a 60-year-old—65% compared to 80%-plus, since maximums are said to drop about a beat per year (from a peak of around 200) after age 25.

Jack Wilmore, exercise physiologist at the University of California in Davis, writes, "From the results of previous studies, it appears that you can obtain a substantial 'conditioning effect' by exercising at a level which is comfortably between 60 and 80% of your capacity. Exercising at a level below 60% results in little, if any, conditioning, and above 80% the gains are small relative to the level of work you are performing."

Wilmore oversees a large adult fitness program at Davis. He tells runners there to go at 75% of their own treadmill-determined maximums. Above 75% running becomes like racing and starts to be uncomfortable. Using Wilmore's standards, few runners would ever want to go higher than a 150 pulse except when racing, and nearly everyone would benefit from rates as low as 120 (60% of 200).

Dr. Samuel Fox, president of the American College of Cardiology, has devised a rule of thumb for determing the highest heart rate at which a fitness-oriented runner should normally go. He simply subtracts age from 170. In practice, a 20-year-old can safely go to 150, a 40-year-old to 130, a 60-year-old to 110.

But here we are getting tangled up in numbers. The point is that each runner listens to the voices inside him. They'll tell him when he's getting too tired from going too fast.

Ernst van Aaken tells runners, "Run playfully in a state of respiratory balance. There must always be—even after hours of training—the desire for and joy in running more, and the ability to do so."

SOCIAL RUNNING

Nine o'clock, Saturday morning. It could be any Saturday of the year, though this happens to be a morning in early fall. The meeting place is the same as always. It's understood that a group will start its run there any Saturday at nine.

The course and distance are never quite the same any two times. But there's always a run—a long, gently-paced run through the campus and the hills to the west. The makeup of the group is never the same two times in a row. Runners come and go. But the group is always there—a group of three or four at least, eight or 10 at most.

We're waiting for George. He'll get here. He's one of the regulars, and he'll come riding up on his bike at five past nine. He always gets here five minutes late. George lives closest of the group's runners. His bike ride is just a mile or so, but it always takes him longest to get here.

Joan hasn't run with us before. She called yesterday and asked, "Can I join you? No one up here wants to go as far as I do, and it's too far for me to go alone." She came the farthest—40 miles—and got here first.

It is agreed only that we'll meet at the same time and place each Saturday, that we'll run two hours and that we'll go only as fast as the slowest runner—except in cases of the slowest having to stop. Then it's understood that someone will drive back over the route later to pick him up. That's the extent of the planning.

The membership of each week's group sets the pace, and the route finds itself. Each session takes on a character of its own. Some runners come to it once and for one reason or another never return. Some come regularly. No one comes every time. No one runner is essential to the life of the group, because the group never stops. Winter and summer, the run goes on.

Common ability and ambitions bind the group. The people who never come back are the ones who can't handle the group's distance and pace. Sometimes it's too slow for them. Sometimes it's too fast. A man came along for a mile or two one Saturday. He was tripping over his feet trying to slow down.

"Can't you pick it up a little?" he pleaded. He heard a chorus of "no's." We haven't seen Phil since.

Today Scott is with us. He doesn't know it yet, and we don't know it, but he's in over his head. It's warm today. Yet he's trying to go twice as far as ever before. He won't even get as far as he has gone before when the walking starts. No one will wait for him, and he won't expect it. That's understood. He won't be back until he's ready.

Five of today's group are getting ready for a marathon at the end of the month. The other two are training for school cross-country season that is about to start. All think that these long Saturday runs are a vital part of their preparation, and that it's easier to do these with company.

The reasons for coming in the first place are practical, even selfish. The reasoning goes like this:

1. Long runs are an important step to my racing goals.

2. They are hard to do alone.

3. Running with a group seems to shorten the miles and shrink the hours.

Practical considerations bring people here. Unique social conditions help keep them coming back week after week. If it weren't for these Saturday morning runs, these people won't mix. They might have a nodding acquaintance at races, but during a race they would run alone regardless of how big the crowd is. Racing demands self-centeredness.

During the week, of necessity, these people run alone and play out the roles that fit their age, profession and sex. But on Saturday mornings, they can all come together, equal and important because they're taking the same run.

John is 14. Vic is 47 and has children older than John. The age spread doesn't draw any lines, nor does the fact that Joan is the only woman among six men.

John and George are in junior high and high school during the week. Vic and Ray work in aerospace science. Joan is a doctor. Scott sells insurance. I'm an editor. But the question, "What do you do?" never comes up on Saturdays. On Saturdays, we are runners.

Ray has been running only six months. I've run longer than everyone else here combined. Only three of us seven have gone as far before as we'll go today. I've gone this far a hundred times or more. But my experience doesn't make the miles any shorter. Only the group can do that. That's why I started coming here.

The Saturday runs are longer than they are hard. We could make them hard, of course, if we wanted to run them fast. But we never do. It's enough just to get through them, and to keep getting through them week after week.

Getting through runs like this is more a matter of patience than pain. Bill, a quarter-miler, had never gone more than eight miles before. One Saturday morning he was training on the track and was feeling bored with it. He saw the group forming. "What's up?" he asked.

"We're taking a long run."

"How long?"

"Two hours."

"What's that in miles?"

"Fifteen or so."

"I can't go that far. But do you mind if I tag along for awhile?"

As we ran, Bill asked, "Do you always run this slow?" It was easy for him, and he went all the way. But his mind wasn't tuned to the distance. He said, "It seemed like we ran all day."

We like to imagine the runs are tough. The hard part is thinking about it for the two hours on the road and in the week between. The group helps people persist during the run and to come back for more, where alone they might have found reasons to stop.

I'm not saying I wouldn't do long weekend runs if it weren't for the group. But I probably wouldn't do as many of them, or go as far. And I'd probably race more often—if only to get out of going long and to have a chance to talk with other runners. But because of the group, the Saturday mornings have come to mean more to me than racing—perhaps because I've run too many races already, and have run too seldom with other people.

More by necessity than choice, I've mostly run alone through the last 16 or 17 years. In high school in a little town in Iowa, no one else ran. There was no track. So I started by running alone on the roads. By college, it was a habit to run this way. No one else wanted to run distance on the roads, so I was still alone in the early 1960s. By the late '60s, road running was the thing to do. Everyone who ran did some of it on the roads. But those who did it were so serious they went too hard and fast for me. Their road runs were like races, so I stayed by myself.

Only in the last couple of years have I fallen in with other runners I can stay with and talk to. I haven't taken five long runs by myself since 1970. Though I still prefer being alone on weekdays, Saturdays are reserved for talking. When I couldn't go long or race for over a year because of my injury, I realized I missed the long runs very much and had little craving for races. Since I've been back, I've

had to choose: long runs or races. They're both on weekends. I haven't run many races and haven't missed many group runs.

After being preached at, argued with, put down and ignored all week—and doing the same from my side—it's nice on Saturday mornings to have a quiet two-way talk. Arthur Lydiard's greatest gift, when he made the long weekend run a standard part of the running diet, was to promote the declining art of conversation. For me, at least, the runs do more good for my social life than my athletic one.

The runners are stripped of their roles and are equal for this couple of hours. There's no need to try and make impressions. The pace has to be slow enough to allow normal breathing. That allows talking. If you can't talk, you're going too fast, Lydiard says. Something about running itself makes runners want to talk. It loosens their tongues more effectively than a third martini. Dr. George Sheehan is positively eloquent when he talks of long run talk:

"Running frees me from the monosyllabic inanities of my usual tongue-tied state, liberates me from the polysyllabic jargon of my profession, removes me from the kind of talk which aims at concealing rather than revealing what is in my heart and what I mean to do and be. For me, no time passes faster than when running with a companion. An hour of conversation on the run is one of the quickest and most satisfying hours ever spent."

Rich, who joins us regularly, is more to the point. He says, "These Saturday mornings are the highlight of my social week. I used to go to parties every weekend before I started running. No more. I don't need them now."

If running with others frees the tongue better than a cocktail party, it also turns loose festering feelings better than a visit to the doctor. For me, these runs have been group therapy in every sense of the word. They've made me whole again.

If it weren't for these sessions, I might have gone on alternately babying my wound, feeling sorry for myself for not being able to run like the other guys, or—worst of all—wearing my scar as a badge of courage and an excuse never to make courageous efforts again.

The group shook those feelings out of me. When we were running and talking, there wasn't time to dwell on my foot the way I did when I was alone. Alone, I felt every step. The first time out with the group, I sometimes forgot the foot for 10 or 20 steps, then a hundred or 200. And finally I wasn't thinking of it at all. I was too busy talking to notice the foot, and it was getting well faster without being watched.

These runs get us outside ourselves, taking our minds off of every single step. And that's good. What's not so good is that we get so busy talking I don't watch where we're going.

This is my home ground. I've been running these country hills for better than 10 years now. So the others let me set the routes. I have an advantage there. I like to take these runs slowly. The others should go slowly, too, but are new here and more eager in this game than I am. They either have to stay with me or run around in circles at each corner shouting back, "Where the hell do we go now?"

But I get to talking and miss turns, or add a mile here or cut off one there because mileage doesn't mean that much to me, or seek out an extra hill on a whim because the hills don't cause me much trouble after all these years.

Today is hot. It was hot when we started, hot and smoggy, and it's getting worse as we go. The temperature is climbing to the 90s, and the air looks and smells like vaporized sewage. The others are losing patience with my guidance. One of those extra hills had done in Scott. When last seen, he was standing at the base of the hill with his hands on his hips, looking up at it and shaking his head.

"Let's get cooled off here," I'd said, pointing to a man hosing down his lawn. Joan had run down the graveled slope first, slipped and sprained her wrist. She is still running.

"How about a detour?" I'd suggested. "It'll only add a couple of miles." Ray and Joan, and of course tireless George, were all for it. We'd just had a water stop. Vic's gaze was vacant. He'd never gone this far this fast. He gave an "it-can't-get-much-worse" nod. Young John, a five-foot 100-pounder running in sneakers, looked bewildered by this whole affair. He figured he had no choice but to go along.

The next series of hills had been on a dusty path that lay exposed to the sun. George had scampered up each of the hills like a frightened llama, then waited with a smug grin at the top. Twice I'd made the mistake of saying, "This is the last hill," and had been wrong.

Ray had said, "If you say that one more time, you're going to get a size 10 Tiger Boston stuffed down your throat."

Now we are lost. Well, not really lost but we're heading west when we should be going east. I know how to get back, but it will add another two miles. Two more miles without water, added to the six since the last drink, makes for testy runners. I think it's time to be quiet.

After running in rare silence for several miles, the group does something rarer yet. It splits in two after an argument over which is the shortest way home and which will have water earliest. When fatigue and thirst set in, it's everyone for himself. Yet it's somehow comforting to have someone to complain with.

We're finally back where we started, and we're already laughing and joking about the run, making it sound worse than it was and saying, "See you next week."

Two sets of opposites put the most strain on the group's integrity. Feeling too good and feeling too bad during the runs themselves. And reaching goals or not reaching them in the races that follow.

People who can't take the Saturday pace drop out. For some, it's too slow, for some it's too fast. But the result is the same. More of them drop out because of goals, because goals are stopping places whether you satisfy them or are frustrated by them.

This run I've talked about came at a crucial time for our group because of the goals involved. The long runs were meant to prepare these runners for the goals. For the schoolboys, George and John, it was the cross-country season. For the rest of us—Joan, Ray, Vic, Scott and me—it was the marathon.

I was interested in seeing how we made out with our goals— whether our Saturday long runs had put us any closer to them. But I was more concerned about what would happen to the group once the goals were out of the way—one way or other.

George turned out to be the best cross-country runner on his high school team and one of the fastest in the city. Last year, he says, he was going "two or three hours a day, but only at 10 or 12 minutes a mile." The group has cut down his distance and picked up his pace, with good results.

John isn't as fragile as he looks in his cut-offs and oversized sneakers. Largely because of his regular long runs, he's one of the top junior high runners in the area. And he'll keep getting better

Joan was worried before the marathon. She'd caught cold. "How do you run a race with a cold?" she asked me. I gave her advice, without even realizing until later that she's the doctor. Cold or not, she was the first woman to finish this race, She ran her best time of 3:17.

Ray hasn't been running long enough to know that a marathoner can't do three hours on six months' preparation. So he almost did it. He ran 3:01 and some odd seconds, and was a little disappointed. "I'd rather have done 3:12 than come this close," he said. He's learning.

In January, Vic had said, "I'll never run in competition." He was talked into trying a *Runner's World* Fun-Run, and has been in competition almost every weekend since. He smiled for 26 miles straight in his marathon and leaped and whooped as he finished. "This was easier than my practice runs," he shouted.

I got through the marathon. I had to walk the last mile, but I made it. I have the group to thank for that. Without the Saturday runs, I would still have been nursing my wounds.

Scott didn't try the marathon. Without the group run that made him face up to his condition, he might have gone in over his head.

Goals met, goals accomplished, or goals thwarted. I wondered how the next week's long run would go. I knew I'd be there, because my only real goal is to keep going. But I wondered how the group would manage to start up again after reaching a stopping place.

Saturday morning, nine o'clock. Seven show up. George, and six of us from the marathon. We have something lasting here.

HARD-EASY, LONG-SHORT

How far is long? How much is distance?

The totals aren't as high as the mile-counters—those who do 200-mile weeks—might have us believe. More is not always, or even often, better. Twice the running will not give twice the return. Counting miles for the sake of counting miles is another dead-end.

Philip Milner writes, "A friend of mine used to run 15 miles Sunday through Friday, and 35 on Saturday... On Saturdays my friend would get up, exercise, spend 3½ hours running his 35 miles, exercise some more, shower, eat a meal and hit the sack for 10 hours sleep. He nearly lost his wife and his health before a leg injury forced him to abandon his quest."

Runners who want to keep going shouldn't be concerned about finding how many miles the human body can tolerate, but in finding its optimum loads. Each new mile beyond the first few yields diminishing returns. Eventually, the miles begin hurting rather than helping.

Hal Higdon, who has run for nearly three decades, was writing some years ago about mercury pollution. "A manufacturer said it costs very little to get 80% of the mercury out of the water," Hal said. "But it costs considerably more to eliminate the next 5%, and an astronomical rate to take out the last little bit. The remaining percentage of mercury, though, can still have serious consequences.

"It's somewhat the same with running. It doesn't take much to get 90% fitness—only a few miles a day. But it takes progressively more training as you get closer to your ultimate potential, until at the highest levels you're putting in a huge investment for a very small gain. It's the small gains, though, that make the difference between winning and losing." It's tempting to invest heavily, in essence to gamble, to win big.

There are ways to gamble without taking too greak a risk, Higdon says. "I read about everyone's training, and there's only one guy who makes any sense. That's Ken Moore, with his 'hard-easy' approach."

Moore wrote in *Road Racers and Their Training,* "I am not a talented runner in the sense of being able to recover from a heavy dose of hard training overnight... I'm not gifted with that amount of adaptive energy. Nor is the majority of distance bugs." So he runs hard one day, then very easily the next two.

"The basis for all training," Moore says, "is that an organism exposed to stress will adjust (get stronger or faster) if allowed to recover. But if it never rests, it just stays tired. I'm not in this to do work. I'm trying to improve. So I'm after the optimum formula of work, rest and racing, not the most difficult I can stand. I've found a dosage of one hard day and two easy brings improvement as quickly as any. It's something every runner must work out for himself."

Hal Higdon says his own perfect way of running would be "methods where I can get the best results from the least effort. I'm not seeing how hard I can work any more, but how little I can get by with." He finds he gets by on a lot less running than he ever thought he could. It simply involves expending Moore's hard-easy idea. They're thinking primarily in daily terms. Hal applies it not only on a daily basis, but also weekly, monthly and even yearly.

This is Higdon's approach: He maintains a good general condition all year, mostly with five or so miles a day of easy running. "But I can pick up easily when I get the urge. I go right into twice-a-day running for a couple of months each year, with lots of mileage and some speed work. Or I run one hard week or workout occasionally. But not constantly hard."

Higdon adds that he quit counting miles a long time ago "because to run high mileage I had to run regularly. I can't hold up to constant pressure, and don't know how much good it really does."

Running hard-easy, long-short, doesn't make for impressive weekly, monthly and yearly mileage totals. But these totals may not rate the value runners have placed on them. Ken Moore says, "I don't view it (mileage) as a valuable indicator of work, and seldom keep track."

There is an inherent trap in high mileages. The only way to get them is by running a lot of miles every day (which can overtax the runner if he doesn't allow himself breaks—which in turn hurt his mileage totals). And the easiest way to get in a lot of miles is to run the same distance every day (which doesn't give the variety that evidence—both psychological and physiological—indicates is essential).

Cliff Temple, a columnist for the British magazine *Athletics Weekly*, has written, "Many distance men have become so obsessed with the sheer quantity of their training that there seems to be an aspect of this way of life that has been overlooked. No, it's not the quality of the training (though it may be too), but the *distribution* of those miles over the week." He advises "not heavier mileage, but redistributed mileage." In other words, a 25-mile day followed by two 5-6-milers, rather than three straight days of 12 miles.

Top British marathoner Tim Johnston says, "The trouble is, one can't help thinking, 'Ah, but if I had trained more I would have run even faster.' In recent years I have gotten in the habit of feeling guilty if I haven't done at least 10 or 15 miles, even on a day that is supposed to be an easy one. No doubt many of us do far more running than we need to, though once you have gotten results on big mileages and have seen others getting them, you are scared to stop. It could well be that it is time to remove the emphasis from miles per week and to concentrate on making the hard days good and hard, and virtually spending the other days in bed."

The only apparent value in mile-counting is as a safety factor— to assure that minimum needs for racing are met, and that long runs don't extend beyond one's trained capacity—which apparently is about three times the daily average.

The Race

4

THE NEED TO RACE

Running and racing use the same action, but they aren't the same in content. Running, gentle running, is a pleasure to do while you're doing it. Racing is painful, and only becomes pleasurable on reflection, after the hurting has stopped. Everyday runs balance themselves between comfortable and uncomfortable. Races operate close to the jagged edge of exhaustion. The trick is to see how close to that edge you can push without falling over.

Distance runner Ona Dobratz says, "With long distances, the body is feeling at home in its environment, functioning as a 'part,' not 'apart.' It's being as one, just as natural as everything around you." But, in contrast, she says racing is "the meshing of mind, body and emotion into complete coordination, not being aware of your surroundings but only of your own movement through space... Just as our voices are not always meant to be calm and want to sing, our legs are not meant always to walk. They want sometimes to run—hard."

The runner running has time and energy to look around. The runner racing has neither. He has to concentrate fiercely on a competition, internal more than external. The demands of the race and the toll of fatigue turn him inside himself.

"Jogging through the forest is pleasant," writes Ken Moore, "as is relaxing by the fire with a glass of gentle Bordeaux and discussing one's travels. Racing is another matter. The front-runner's mind is filled with an anguished fearfulness, a panic, which drives him into pain."

"Exploring the forest is easy," Moore says. "Exploring the limits of human performance is excruciating." The runner who only runs comfortably sees only the flat and quiet forest floor. The racer seeks out the valleys and peaks of himself.

Despite all the logical reasons not to race, runners keep racing. The challenge is there, and they need to wallow in it. They need to know what's inside themselves, to tear themselves down a bit to see what they have built up.

Jock Semple, the colorful organizer of the Boston marathon, thinks compulsive racers are like impatient farmers. Racing, he says, "is like pulling up the carrots to see if they're growing."

SPEED RUNNING

The biggest race ended sometime between midnight and dawn on Sunday morning. Anything the marathon had to offer after that couldn't have been as bad as what the weather would have offered had it not changed. Northern California had been broiling for days. Five days before the marathon, the air-conditioning switched off. The ocean breeze died. Whisky-brown smog hovered about. The air heat up, pushing close to 100.

The hot spell had started early enough that it might break by Sunday. It would be a close thing, but the weather might change. If it changed, the switch would be fast and delightful. Saturday afternoon the waves of heat still danced up from the highway. Dirty air smudged out the view of the mountains on both sides of the Napa Valley. The Volkswagen dealer's time-temperature sign read "5:45" then "96."

"I'm not running," I told my wife Janet. I'd made up my mind a long time ago that I wouldn't try any more hot-weather marathons. These runs are hard enough without the heat riding along on my shoulders. There's no percentage in it. In the heat, the effort is greater for a slower time.

The recent unpleasantness with my heel had taught me it's often better to leave races alone than to bull through them. The suffering isn't worth enduring. I'd been enjoying a period of super-health since recovering from the surgery and I didn't want to blow the feeling now.

I'd solved one riddle of nature when it was almost too late to put the new knowledge to use. I'd learned how often I could safely race. The code had always been there, but I had to break myself down before I could break it. In the time since I'd switched to slower running, I'd spent three years living within the code. Then two more years violating it with reckless naivete. And two more years trying to figure out why I was spending more time in doctors' offices than on the road. I'd looked back to 1968, one of the good years, to see if I could reclaim its lessons.

Ah, 1968. I didn't know why and it wasn't planned that way, but everything was right in my running then. I had two speeds—easy and all-out—and apparently had stumbled onto the right balance between the two.

ed to the country, where every day's run was a quiet,
ed one. My peace of mind never registered higher. I
g much, but the races run were good ones. Most of them
or the "slow" phase of my life—a few were bests ever.
e was nothing super, but I didn't seem to need more. It
was steady, and that's what counted. There was no interruptions
for injuries and illnesses. That was both because of the way I ran
and the *cause* of the way I raced.

The "code" of that model year, as best as I can tell, is 2-10%.
That means I feel best and race best when only 2-10% of my total
running is race-like. The other 90-98% is just steady, easy, unstruc-
tured running. The reason for the strict racing limit—no more than
one-tenth of the time—is that races hurt. They tear down what the
realxed everyday running has built up. So hard running has to have
controls put on it.

When I checked my own racing percentages, the figures gave
a clear picture of what had happened. I listed every month since
starting slow running in 1966, dividing total running time by the
time spent racing. (I keep my records by time instead of distance,
but the percentages work out about the same the other way.) The
resulting "codes" told me almost exactly how I felt and how I raced
that month. Under 10% usually meant fresh and fast. Over 10%
meant weary and slow, or worse. The "or worse" is what I was
most concerned about.

In 1968, I ran best times at everything from one mile to 18-
plus miles. I was healthy and fast without knowing why. Now I
know why. I can see it in the racing percentages. The whole year
averaged 6% racing. The best two months—July and December—
were 3% and 2%.

The next year, 1969, stayed pretty good. There were good
times, but injuries and illnesses as well. The overall racing total
was 6%, but that's deceiving because I didn't race at all on two of
those months. I came down with bronchitis late in the year—after
a 13% monthly binge.

This was the start of a long period of escalating racism. As I
got sick and hurt, I wondered if gentle running was failing me. It
took three years to realize that this trouble was coming not from
the slow running, but too much too fast too often.

In 1970, I raced 14% of the time. In the first 10 months of
1971, the figure was 18%. Racing ability slipped first. I was too
tired to race well. Minor injuries grew into major ones. In 1970, I
pulled a calf muscle in the third straight month over 10%. A year

later, I hurt my achilles tendon in the second month over *20%*.

The achilles problem was a bad one. It knocked me out for almost three months. But I didn't learn anything from it, coming right back with 11% and 15% months. Then bursitis started. Even while it was hurting, I did 23% in May 1972. That did it. It was a year and an operation before I raced again. This would be the first marathon since then. But it was one I could skip if necessary. No race now was too good to miss.

I'd written off the Napa race as soon as we saw the time-temperature sign at the edge of town. It wasn't so much of a loss, really. I hadn't done anything special for this. No buildup or taper in my daily runs. No high-starch diet. I didn't even have a time goal or race plan.

This wasn't any kind of end for me. It was just a checkpoint on the road to getting fit again. An important checkpoint, yes, but it could wait a month or two months or more. The heat didn't disappoint me for myself so much as for the half-dozen or so others in our Saturday morning group who'd plotted this out like a military campaign and were about to march into a cruel ambush.

"Just wait," Janet said on Saturday night. "Tomorrow will be cool and foggy." She's a life-long Californian and knows the pattern.

First thing Sunday morning, I threw back the drapes to look out on the day. Mist was dripping from the heavy gray blanket that had rolled in from the west while we slept.

"Look!"

"Didn't I tell you?" Janet smiled.

The biggest race was over. I knew then that the run would take care of itself, following patterns that were just as predictable as California's weather. I've been through those patterns enough times to know them. Yet they always surprise me a little when they go again just as they should. One of the lasting and consistent mysteries is pace. Each race has a pace of its own, and I can never guess in advance what it's going to be. It has to find itself.

There's a lot to be said for not knowing. Innocence isn't always ignorance but is often an intuitive kind of wisdom. It's one step above the rational kind of knowledge involved in laying out plans of time over distance and trying to follow them to the number.

I've had trouble when I've drawn plans that combined time and distance and have known what the two are and mean every minute and mile. This kind of plan breeds tension. It puts in the conscious mind things that are better left to unconscious wisdom.

I used to time all my daily runs, always running them on measured courses. The full set of records looked good in my books, but didn't comfort me much as I ate away at my health. I still time my daily runs. But there's a difference. I make it a point *not* to know how far they are. That way there's no reason to hurry or worry. I use time to tell me how long I've been out. It's a handy way to keep track. But time can't use me as its competitor every day.

Races are different. I want to go fast there. But I've found I can go fastest when I don't think about doing it. When I don't have a preset schedule of pace or split times to remind me of what I am or would be doing. The race has a set distance which I want to run as fast as I can manage it. But I don't want to know how fast that is until I'm finished.

On race days, tension is lowest when I run distance without time. Other signs than pace per mile, better voices than the harsh, cold shout of the timer tell me how I am and should be running. The voices from inside are soft and sensitive. If listened to and pampered, they respond beautifully. Distance and times have their place as records of what has happened. But they get in the way of pace while it's happening.

The race has to set a pace for itself. In marathons, I'm afraid to guess what it might be for fear of scaring me out of trying it. For some reason, I can go two minutes a mile faster for two or three times the distance that I normally run. It happened at Napa. I'd been averaging just six or so miles of running a day in recent weeks, probably at no faster than eight or 8½ minutes a mile. And here I was feeling fresh and strong after almost 2½ hours of close to 6½ minute-paced running.

Ten minutes later, I was running 8½-minute miles. And a half-hour later, I wasn't running at all. The race was still on, but I was walking. Couldn't help it. I'd gone past my "collapse point." It was as simple as that. It had nothing to do with gutlessness or with stupid pacing. I'd simply gone past my capacity.

I'd learned about "collapse" since the last marathon. The theory is that, under the best conditions of weather and pacing, a runner's fuel supplies will stretch to three times his average daily run for the last couple of months. I knew about it, but hadn't insured myself against collapse.

I'd done 50 minutes a day in August and September. The best I could hope for, according to the theory, was 2½ hours of strong

running. At a few minutes before that deadline, I felt so strong I was accelerating. I wasn't psyched out by a theory. In fact, I was thinking, "This doesn't apply to me today. Today I'm going to cheat 'collapse' out of a victim."

There was a little hill. A mile or two earlier, I wouldn't have noticed it. Now suddenly, it became very hard. I plodded and wheezed up it. I came on my lon-run partner Ray. He had collapsed and was walking.

"How far from here?" I asked him. When I have to ask the question, I know I'm in trouble.

Collapse isn't as awful as it sounds. It isn't as painful as the rigor mortis that sets in during the deep oxygen debt of a mile. By the time collapse comes, you're numbed enough that you hardly feel it. Oh, you know it's there by the fact that the pace all at once has slowed by two minutes a mile. You know because distance and time are distorted out of all sensible proportion. A half-hour and 3½ miles may as well be five hours and 50 miles, as long as they sound.

The head is fairly clear yet, but the legs, from the big muscles in the hips that pick them up to the tiny muscles in the big toe which drive off the ground are so drained of fuel that they can't lift any more. They don't scream. They simply balk like a stubborn woman and say quietly but firmly, "You've abused me long enough. I can't take it any more. I can't and I won't." And that's that.

Once collapse comes, it is final. You don't pull out of it—not in the remaining distance, and not for days afterwards. This is the predictable result of going too far. The only way to avoid it is by taking on extra fuel in the weeks and months before. "Extra fuel" means enough background running. There aren't any service stations for collapsed runners in the last three miles of a marathon.

The little hill there at 23 miles loomed mountain-like in front of me. Ray couldn't have been moving faster than eight-minute miles, yet he was moving away.

"Just keep moving," I said to myself, almost as a chant in rhythm with my slowing steps. "Just keep moving, no matter how slow it gets. "If I can keep jogging, I'll be happy."

By 25 miles, even that was impossible. I started walking. I walked all the way to the last quarter-mile, where pride triumphed over tiredness for two awful minutes.

I didn't care, when it was over, that I had walked. The rest of the race had been too good to be spoiled by that ending. I'd run 23 miles so much better than expected that I could have stopped there and been happy. Doing the rest of it at all could only make me happier.

"But if you'd run in, you could have broken three," someone said. That's like saying, "If you'd run faster, you would have broken 2:30." Or why not 2:15?

I did what I could and had no complaints. As it was, what I *could* do was more than I *should have done.* My knee hurt and it hurt for a long time to come.

The knee started hurting after the "collapse point" in the marathon. "It's just a little thing," I told myself. And within a week I was back to normal distances. I kept to my regular plan of hours on Tuesdays and Thursdays, two hours on Saturdays and half-hours the rest of the days. This had evolved into my weekly plan. I thought I had to keep to it. It was too rigid. The knee didn't get any better.

I was working then on the booklet *Exercises for Runners.* It is mostly about how to keep the feet and legs in good working order. It's a calm, rational, easily-understood guide to preventive medicine. The advice is sound.

I typed: "Those who write about running are just like anyone else who runs. They don't worry much about what they don't have wrong with them. They don't often practice preventive medicine, but only go looking for solutions to problems as pain makes itself felt. Pain demands relief, and in that way is an effective teacher."

I wrote this before the pain was to the point where it was forcing me to heed the words that were going down on paper.

"...not much of the experience seems to sink into the reader until he himself is faced with a similar situation and pain demands that he re-read the old article."

Soon a cramping pain was locking up my left kneecap before I'd gone two miles. I was rereading my own writing and paying attention this time.

"... the worst kinds of injuries are those which hurt more as you run. Some pains gradually disappear. Others grow worse. You can usually run safely through the first type. But you have to be ready to stop for the second. Growing pain is a stop sign."

That makes sense. Aggravating an injury isn't going to make it get better. Half of the book is about stretching exercises. These exercises are based on yoga. And yoga is based on the concepts of no strain and no pain.

The advice from yoga is "stretch only to the point where pain is felt, then back off slightly and hold that position. Nothing is gained from pushing past the point of discomfort."

"Stretch, don't strain," the yogis say again and again in the book. The message for my running should have been obvious, if I'd been looking for advice instead of giving it.

Nothing is gained in running, either, by plunging day after day into the pain zone. The pains have no choice but to get worse when I do this. The way out is the yoga way. Run only to the point of obvious discomfort, then back off a few steps and hold that level.

The book that I reread because of my sore knee says, " As long as the demands of the body are moderate but regular, the flexibility to accomplish the extreme positions comes with time. It may be a long time coming, but don't rush it. People who hurry in yoga get hurt. One has to work within his own limitations and progress at his own rate."

Change "flexibility" to "endurance fitness," "positions" to "distances" and "yoga" to "running" and this is the best paragraph of advice I could give myself.

Giving advice and following it are, of course, two different things. I give it all the time through the magazines and booklets. But I don't face up to the truth of these things myself until I have no other way to look. The knee pain was more an irritant than an injury at first, grinding away just above the level of consciousness. I pretended nothing was wrong. I clung to my pre-determined schedule. I had my own ideas about how long to run. In this case, they were in conflict with the time that knee should have been running just then.

I said an hour. It said 40-45 minutes.

I ran my hour. The knee's limit dropped to 35 minutes.

I ran my weekend two hours. The next day the trouble began after only 20 minutes. That got me to thinking about being more flexible.

Flexibility. That's the key word in running health. This is the key concept in the exercise book. It says that maybe half of the injuries that runners get are the result of being too tight. Tight muscles lead to tight tendons and cartilages and joints that get sore when they're jerked excessively.

The way to counteract this tightness is to stretch gently with yoga-like exercises. I do these. And I still get pains like the one in my knee. This is because I'm still inflexible. It's another kind of inflexibility that's harder to see. It's the one that accounts for almost all the injuries that aren't caused by muscle tightness.

This is rigidity of mind. It's a stubborness that makes some runners think they have to go six minutes every mile, or 100 miles every week, or in my case an average of an hour every day. It's a schedule hangup that leads to trouble when any weakness is present. A man has to stretch himself or he won't get anyplace. But an important part of stretching is knowing when to stop.

Stop at the point of pain—not the fatigue-related pain that is sometimes part of running, but the chronic injury type of pain which obviously is foreign.

Another line I typed once and then forgot: "Be like water, which is not firm, hard and unyielding but rather seeks the lowest place—and yet can wear down the hardest stone."

As soon as I quit rolling like a stone and started flowing like a stream, the knee recovered within weeks.

RACING AND SURVIVING

A runner who wants to race *has* to race. It's both a psychological urge and a physical necessity.

George Young, one of the world's most competitive over-35-year-olds, has said, "There's no better way to get in speedwork than running a race. You talk of speedwork in terms of quarters and all those other things. But you don't get the speedwork (there) that you gain in a race. You never really reach the pain barrier, or whatever you call it, in any other way than running the race and hurting that way."

Racing is going beyond oneself and one's imagined limits, and the race is the only place this can be conveniently done. But coming to a racing peak also puts one on the brink of exhaustion, illness and injury.

George Sheehan has written, "The story is a familiar one whenever coaches and runners talk about the mysteries of running. A personal best performance, another push to the limits, and then disaster. Being at absolute peak is just one step from losing it all... The urge toward excellence can breed biological arrogance, a feeling that you are superior to the laws of nature."

In a reader survey, *Runner's World* found that three-fourths of the responding runners were racers at one level or another. Two-thirds of the 1700 had suffered serious injury at some point in their careers. *RW* compared the healthy with the injured runners. There was little difference in the length of time they'd been running. The healthy group had been in the sport slightly more time. These people ran slightly less mileage, on the average, than the injured ones, did less running on the hard roads and had more frequent rest days. But the differences weren't too significant.

Racing separated them. Of the injured group, 97% were racers. The percentage among the healthy group was 37%. The majority of the injured runners competed more than once a month, while the bulk of the healthy ones raced less than monthly. The healthy runers also were slower. Only one in six of them had broken five minutes in the mile, three hours in the marathon or the equivalent at other distances. One in two of the injured ones had run at least this fast, indicating they took their racing more seriously.

The high injury figures hint that racing as presently carried out is more a foolhardy risk than a calculated one. Racers apparently either lack the guidelines that can make their racing relatively safe or they ignore them.

Paul Slovic, author of a detailed statistical study of marathon runners, says, "The amazing thing about this tremendous expenditure of time and effort (in preparing for races and running them) is that most of it is fashioned without benefit of sound factual evidence. Intuition and hearsay, mixed with imitation, eventually modified by personal and sometimes painful experience, serve to shape the runner's program."

Through trial-and-error groping, runners slowly are refining the techniques of preparing for racing. They center on three broad areas.

● **Training background**—How much mileage does a runner need and for how long a period, simply to finish a race?

● **Race-spacing**—How much time does a runner need between races to recover and rebuild adequately?

● **Seasonal peaking**—How long does it take to reach top racing form, and how long can it be maintained once gained?

The first two points apply to long distance runners, the last to shorter distance runners. Together they give a clearer picture of how to maximize results and minimize risks.

BACKGROUND

How much background mileage? Ken Young's "collapse point" theory gives a clue. Young, an ultra-marathon racer, says the point at which one breaks down in a long distance race will be about one-twentieth of his total mileage for the past two months.

In other words, if you logged 400 miles during that period and you're trying to race a marathon, you can figure to be in trouble after 20 miles. Twenty miles is one-twentieth of 400. Young uses two months' running as a basis because he says that's how long it takes to accumulate the desired training effect.

There's a simpler way to express Young's formula and yet not tamper with its basic premise. Reduce the mileage (or the total time if you keep record that way) to a daily average. Tripling that average gives the same collapse point as Young's original method.

The practical significance is this: If you want to finish a race before the physical resources run dry, plan on averaging at least one-third of the race distance (or time) per day for eight or more weeks before the race. Beyond the collapse point lurks not only slowdowns and dropouts, but potential injuries from severely depleted reserves.

A common average for marathoners is 50 miles a week. That's seven each day. Triple that, and the collapse point is 21 miles. Ken Young doesn't think it is coincidence that "so many low-mileage runners hit the wall around 20 miles of a marathon."

Ken says, "I would emphasize that these are basically absolute minimums. You can't expect to go farther than the collapse distance even under the *best* conditions (of pace, terrain and weather). And under typical conditions, you may collapse before this point. Also, if the collapse point is close to the racing distance, the runner is only going to be able to cover the distance *without collapsing*. This does not mean he is going to be able to race *well* at six miles, for example, by maintaining two miles a day. He will just be able to cover six miles."

Paul Slovic provides authoritative statistical backing for Young's theory. Slovic found in a detailed statistical study of several hundred marathoners that those who slowed down least in the late stages of the race ran best. And those who had more substantial mileage backgrounds held up best toward the end.

The entire field at Seaside, Ore., in 1973 averaged 42 miles a week, or six a day, according to Slovic. This was in the eight weeks before the late February race. But the men finishing faster than three hours were doing about nine miles a day—compared to five miles for the slower runners. The sub-three group had a projected collapse point of 27 miles; the over-threes could expect trouble after 15 miles.

Slovic matched pace for the first 10 miles against the last six-plus. All runners slowed somewhat. But in the sub-three-hour group the slowdown averaged 14% while in the lighter trainers it was almost three times as great—40%! Slovic separated the runners breaking 2:45. They trained 10 miles a day, putting their collapse point farther beyond marathon distance. The average drop in pace for these runners was only 8½%.

Ken Young says the collapse point can be pushed back, and the fastest, least painful way to do it is to begin at the bottom. He tried going from the top, frequently going as far as he was able and then trying to labor on.

"It took me two years to increase my collapse point from 20 to 30 miles using this method," he says. "But since realizing the correlation between total mileage and collapse, I've added roughly

20 miles to my collapse point in 1½ years." He did so by upping his average.

RACE-SPACING

Racers build to destroy. Runners preparing for races are like children building sand castles. They work long and carefully on the building. Then, swoosh! A hard race rolls in like a wave to level the project. Then they carry away the remains to start building again.

Racing is as destructive as it is rewarding. Sometimes the destruction is slow and subtle. Sometimes it is quick and violent. But there's always some tearing down of what has been built so carefully.

The trick is (1) building faster than destroying; (2) confining most of the hurting to race days and not racing on days when hurting before the start; (3) spacing races so damage is more than repaired in between them.

The answer to race-spacing may be a formula: Race no more than 10% of the total mileage. This recommendation isn't strictly personal and arbitrary. It's based on advice of two highly respected coaches. German Ernst van Aaken and New Zealander Arthur Lydiard have proposed racing quotas ranging from 2-10%. These limits may or may not apply to everyone. The best way to find your own limits is to keep your own records. Match gentle running against hard running, reducing the race-like work to a percentage of the total. That way you can look back and see what you were doing when you were healthy and hurt, sharp and dull, fresh and tired, and you can find correlations.

Your border line might not be 10%. But somewhere in there you're going to spot three points:

● **Minimum sharpness**—If you're racing, you need a specific kind of preparation that only racing can give. A certain small percentage is essential. Otherwise, you'll feel sluggish and awkward when you try to go hard.

● **Best racing**—This is the ideal balance. You're sharp, but you're not draining yourself too much. This is where the best races lie.

● **The limit**—The most you can race without inflicting long-term damage.

Ten percent may be an outside figure for everyone if it is for a runner whose other work is strictly low-stress. Five percent may be a more likely limit for faster trainers, whose training resembles racing. And 2% might be enough for those who hit speedwork regularly.

We're talking about recovery and rebuilding here. You don't need foxy formulas or high math to insure that the interval between races is adequate. Say you've found from experience that 5% is your best level. Okay, simply multiply your racing distance by 20. Don't run another race until you've gone that far. If it is a five-mile race, take 100 miles to rebuild. Or you can work it out by time. If the race lasts 30 minutes, run 600 minutes or 10 hours before the next one. It all works out about the same.

A California high school coach has used this kind of guideline for years. Tom Gleason of Lancaster won't let his cross-country runners race again until they've logged 100 training miles. The racing percentage under this system works out to less than 5%.

Gleason said in 1973, "We have had only one injury in the last two years. That was when a kid tripped over a fence he was trying to jump."

Two self-adjustments are built into the formula. Theoretically the more one is accustomed to running, the quicker he recovers. The percentage allows a high-mileage runner to compete more often than a light trainer. And, in theory, the mile doesn't demand nearly as much recovery time as a marathon. So miles can be raced more often.

Even on the high side of the formula, though, there isn't room for a lot of racing. This is as it should be, because you can run into big trouble by doing too much and there's little chance of doing too little. Racing dullness is easily corrected. Racing injuries aren't.

Too many good races can add up to bad racing in the long run. And a bad race can be a good early warning of trouble, begging to be corrected before it multiplies. Racing is two-faced. It is fun and satisfying and it is a beast that has to be kept caged. There are ways to make the most of it with the least threat:

1. Race seldom, but regularly and well.

2. Plan number, type and pace with extreme care.

3. Race within trained capacity. This means staying well within the collapse point of three times the average daily distance or time.

4. Take no half-measures. Either race or don't race. If you're putting in race-type investment of effort, you want and deserve race type return. Save "speedwork" for races.

5. There is no need for special pseudo-races or speedwork if

racing opportunities are adequate. Racing quotas are best met in races, where hard running counts.

6. If there aren't enough chances to race, sharpen with runs that look and feel like races. "Controlled" time-trials, at, say, 90-95% speed are one way.

7. Racing sharpness is specific. Miles take a different kind of stress than marathons. Best results come from racing close to a specific distance for a period of time.

8. The longer the distance raced, the less often you race. Following the percentages takes care of that automatically.

9. After long periods away from racing, allow a "sharpening" race or two (or more). It's normal to feel slow and sluggish at first. Be patient.

10. Don't fight nature. Don't race when tired or sore. If you're that way before the start, think what the hard miles are going to do later.

PEAKING

Racing energies rarely flow evenly. They warm and cool as the seasons do—often in tune with those seasons. Traditionally, in the United States at least, running has been a moderate-weather sport: track in the spring, cross-country in the fall. As indoor track, summer competition and road racing have exploded, though, racing has oozed out to all corners of the year. Racing is never out of season.

With proper race spacing, this need not give long distance racers problems. If races are spaced adequately, seasons take care of themselves. You race, then take a recovery-rebuilding break that lasts from weeks to months.

Shorter distance runners, however, can race as often as every few days and still be within race-spacing limits. They can continue racing this way year-round. But should they? Available evidence indicates they should not. Instead, they should race for a few months then back off to rebuild.

The year needs a focus, a peak period, and it also needs a building phase. This is a central theme of Arthur Lydiard, the well-traveled and successful coach from New Zealand.

"You can't race well the year-round," Lydiard says, "because your condition will only take you so far. When you're racing hard, you can't train hard. If you compromise, you can hold your form for three or four months. But (then) you're going to have to go back and start to build up again."

Lydiard's influence is evident in the current generation of Finnish runners. Lydiard coached there in the late 1960s. Though not coached directly by him, Lasse Viren echoes Lydiard's peaking philosophy—except that Viren sets tighter time limits. He said after winning the 10,000 and 5000 at Munich Olympics the, "Top shape can be planned and timed fairly accurately and, at least in my case case, top shape will stay for a period of about three weeks. It is not possible to conserve good form for a long time in distance running. My first important race of 1972 was the 10,000 meters in Munich."

Statistics from world class athletes support the peaking plan. *Runner's World* analyzed the season records of world ranked men and women from one year. Four factors were checked: (1) total number of races during the year; (2) race in which the best time was run; (3) months between the first and last race; (4) months from the first to the fastest race.

These figures indicated how long and how many races it took to reach peak form, and how this compared to the total length of the season. Results:

1. The total number of races during the year was five for middle-distance runners (800-10,000 meters) and three for long distance athletes.

2. Regardless of event, racers reached peak form after about three-fifths of their season—in the third of five races, for instance.

3. The length of the season (first to last race) ranged from 2½ to four months.

4. In all groups, peak racing came either late in the second month or racing or early in the third.

Two conclusions come from these figures:

● There's no substitute for racing as a sharpener. Most runners need from two to five races at their main racing distance before getting their best times. This specific conditioning apparently is best achieved with a 6-8-week period.

● This peak, once achieved, doesn't last very long. And most racers continue beyond it. They typically race twice in the month and a half after peaking.

Slipping performance, Tom Osler, says, is the first sign of energy depletion. "One can rarely maintain a high performance level for more than three months," according to Osler. "(Heavy racing) must therefore be terminated after about three months or when symptoms of energy depletion are first observed."

He calls for a return to the seasonal racing tradition, which more or less corresponds with nature's seasonal cycle. Osler thinks runners tend to work in six-month cycles—three months high and three low. Each year has two high seasons and two low, two for sowing (background training) and two for reaping (racing).

The Ideal

MILES FROM NOWHERE

If you were on a high school or college track team as recently as a year ago, count the number of your teammates who are still running. If you have to figure higher than 10%, your school is most unusual. Your coach has planted a wonderful seed of interest in his athletes. This doesn't happen in most schools, which account for all but a small percentage of US runners—and therefore most of the dropouts each graduation day.

Hal Higdon has been running most of the years since leaving school, and probably will keep running the rest of his life. Hal recalls his college class' 20-year reunion. "Three or four classmates came up to announce that they were doing some running themselves," Hal says. "But the thing that really struck me was that the current runners from the class of 1953 were not the athletes. They were the non-athletes who seemed to have discovered this thing later in life. None of them had been on the track team. The one former track man I saw there does no running at all. Maybe this says something about our sport."

It says several things. For one, Hal Higdon is the exception and his former teammate the rule. Few runners continue, and the reasons for quitting are many. Some runners are discouraged by unfulfilled goals, some are satisfied by fulfilled ones, some are disabled by chronic injuries, and some are unable or unwilling to make room among their responsibilities for running.

If you're running to last, it may be best *not* to set high goals for yourself. Goals are stopping places when they relate to racing performance. People stop when they fall short of them, and often when they reach them. The only goal should be to keep going. To keep going, you have to keep healthy, happy and hungry. You have to get your kicks from the means, not some imagined end.

The pursuit of excellence is so fast and hard that runners who choose this route don't often stay on it for long—"long" in this case meaning 10, 20 or more years, with no desire to stop. Pursuing excellence means suffering, sacrificing and gambling. It isn't easy to keep doing any of these unless a person keeps meeting his high standards, and it is all but impossible to meet these standards year after year.

One long-term racer is quoted in the booklet *Racing Techniques* as saying, "You have to look at your career as if it's a race, then pace yourself accordingly. If you're planning to run indefinitely, you don't blow everything by sprinting the first mile. You find a pace that you can comfortably carry all the way. One year to me is like the first mile of a marathon, and I have to be careful not to go out too fast."

Long running is a matter of pacing. A miler can't go at sprinters' pace, and a marathoner can't run like a miler. That's obvious. Pacing is also a weekly, monthly, yearly, *careerly* concept. This isn't so obvious, but perhaps is more crucial to long-run health, happiness and running appetite.

Runners have a clear choice: go hard, fast and short, or go easy, slow and long. It works that way in individual runs and over the long haul. The runners who go hardest and fastest usually reap the biggest success. But their pace also kills them off early. Runners who go easy and slow aren't likely to win much. But their more casual pace keeps them going. They don't have to run very hard to beat people who have dropped out.

This isn't to suggest that gentle pacers can't be fast some of the time, have high-level success for awhile and still enjoy decades of running. It's just a warning against suffering, sacrificing and gambling *all* the time. The odds are against those who try that.

The secret of a long running life is summed up in six words from Larry Lewis: "Keep moving and don't fight yourself."

Keep moving. Lewis said, "The minute I hear a man say he's going to lie in the sun and enjoy his retirement, I know he's about to meet his maker." Larry died at 106. He'd run for 97 of those years, and up to a couple of months before his death.

Don't fight yourself. There's no winner. If a man has himself as an enemy, who does he look to as a friend?

The runner who keeps going is one who is friendly with himself, who grows and adapts to changing conditions as he goes, and whose greatest pleasure is in where he is, not in where he has been or where he is headed.

Runners who want to go long can take a hint from Robert Louis Stevenson, who wrote, "I travel not to go anywhere, but to go." Look not for someplace to stop, but ways to keep going.

RUNNING THROUGH TIME

We call it a river, though I see now it is barely creek-size. East of my hometown in Iowa, across the railroad tracks, Highway 208 and Elmer Harris' corn field, runs what the map calls the East Tarkkio River.

We call it "Tarkey," "The Tark," or just "The River." It was very much a part of my growing up. Between the earliest age I can remember and about 15, I sepnt all my summer days and a lot of other ones in, on or beside it. It seemed like a big river then, and a long way to it. But I wasn't very big myself, and my perspective was still Coin, Iowa, scale. Coin had 330 people then, all living within a square mile.

None of the three bridges was more than a mile's walk from home. They were named for their paint jobs—the Pink Bridge north of town, the Green Bridge due east and the Silver down south. The paint colors eventually changed, but the names stayed the same. The Green was the closest but the dullest place to go. The Pink had the best swimming holes but was the longest walk. The Silver was the best for fishing, and we could walk the railroad tracks to it.

We swam The River there in the summer and skated in the winter, pulled fish from it and floated on it—from the Pink down to the Silver Bridge on rubber inner-tubes, dug caves in its banks and dirtied its water. The River survived us, as it has survived generations of little boys before and since.

The East Tarkio River never looked the same two days and two places in a row. It was always changing. That was a part of the fascination with it.

After a violent thunderstorm, the kind southwest Iowa gets regularly, the river ran wild. The muddy rampage rose almost to bridge level. On days like this, we scurried out to the Green Bridge to watch in amazement, chuck in rocks, boards, garbage, anything we could find. We hoped it would spill out its banks, across Elmer Harris' field to lap up against the highway at the edge of town. It had never happened in my time, but I'd heard stories that sustained hopes.

During the hot summer dry spells, The Tarkey dried to a trickle, shallow enough to wade across and so clear we could see fish gasping for water. It never dried up completely.

In winter, the River froze over. But under the suspended surface of snow and ice, water kept gurgling until the spring thaw.

After washing itself clean from the floods or satisfying its thirst or shaking off the cold, The River meandered lazily in its banks. Most times it acted like this. Beaver dams went up and came down along the channel. Swimming holes were dug and filled. The shoreline shifted. New sets of little boys grew up in, on and beside it, and then grew up and left home. The River rolled on. It goes on now, like a relay runner, taking water from surrounding creeks and later handing it off to a bigger river downstream, passing life along.

I was back in Coin not long ago and went to the Green Bridge to have a nostalgic look. It had been many years since I'd played there. It was the same, and it was different. It was smaller, but I had been the one who had changed, not The River. There was more garbage under the bridge than I had remembered, but maybe I was just more aware of it now. Old walls had crumbled. New bends in the course had formed.

But The River itself was rolling along as it always had, patiently adapting to changing times and conditions. That's why it has lasted so long. That river had something to say to a runner, though the lesson had been lost in me until a Chinese running friend pointed it out.

Bill Yee signs his letters, "The Mystic of the Redwoods." Thanks to his ancestry, he has a rich strain of Eastern philosophy still running through him. But sometimes his passive mysticism gets diluted by Western ambition. Occasionally I stumble onto a bit of mysticism.

Bill happened to get ambitious on the same day I got mystical, and we learned from each other. I did most of the learning. He already knew these things, but needed to have them reinforced by experience.

We were running a marathon in the northern California redwoods. I told Bill beforehand, "I'm not going to race it. I'm just going to enjoy the trees." I wasn't playing games with him. I meant it. I had no serious intentions. If it went well, fine. If it didn't, I still had the scenery.

There's only one person who can beat me, and that's me. I've tried to quit worrying about the finish of races, because that's the surest way to beat myself. I just think about how I'm going to start—which is easily and unambitiously. When I say I'm starting that way, I'm not trying to fool anyone, but only trying to avoid

fooling myself. Later on, in the second half of the race, I can work if all the signs say go. Illusions will have vanished by then. There's nothing mystical about this. It's a practical, self-preservation thing.

This time I breezed past Bill at 15 miles, running comfortably. I still didn't intend to "race" this redwoods marathon and wasn't racing against Bill. I was trying to get through it as best I could. It just happened that I got through it quicker than he did. I saw nothing in my race more subtle than that. But "The Mystic of the Redwoods" had a different version of the race. This is what mysticism is—an uncommon view of common   things.

Bill Yee: "Your approach to racing is a wise one. I can see a philosophical basis for it. Your 'I'm not going to race this one' is a beautiful ploy. You always finish before me regardless.

"Your intention before the race *is* not racing. Maybe once you get going the momentum, rhythm, elation and primitive kinesthetic joy in the running sweeps you along into a 'competition' of sorts. But not the cut-throat, dog-eat-dog, self-centered type of competition encouraged by the American tradition.

"This approach to racing is related to the Taoist concept of never being ambitious. Be like water, which is not firm, hard and unyielding, but rather seeks the lowest places—and yet can wear down the hardest stone.

"I can see I have limited my potential by being too ambitious, by striving too hard. In my misguided ambition, I set up three hours as an abstract, arbitrary goal to achieve, to strain and gasp after— which is the antithesis of Taoist values.

"I *know* I am a sub-three-hour marathoner. I'll run under that time sooner or later. It is useless to strain after it like it were grapes before the fox. I'll run my 2:58 someday when I've just gone out relaxed, with the intention of having an enjoyable run—not intending to blast three hours by sheer blood and guts. I'll go out relaxed and easy and let the competitive instinct build up naturally—a groundswell of elation and exhilaration."

No use worrying. By the time the race comes, it's too late to change anything. The water is in the stream, or as they say back home in Iowa "the hay is in the barn." And wishing and pushing aren't going to make the resources any richer. The capacity to race is set not by what you think and do while racing but by the background running that has come before. What's going to happen is going to happen, and what's not is not. So you might as well relax and take it as it comes.

Be like water, Bill Yee says. Ebb and flow. Fill the reservoir in long, steady, gentle, regular runs. Then when time comes to race, just open the tap and let the stored water flow.

If you've stored well, you'll race well. If not, forget it. You can't pump water from a dry hole. Turn around and refill the reservoir. Filling is the easy and fun part. It means gathering gentle, almost effortless mileage. Filling is the easy part. Man, like the river, has to keep moving or he dries up. But that doesn't imply that draining it is neccessarily like the breaking rocks. There's some effort to it, sure. But it's inevitable effort. As the water level rises, it almost must fall. It has to come out somehow.

LIKE THE RIVERS

"The philosophy of Lao Tzu is simple," say the editors of his Vintage book *Tao Te Ching.* "Accept what is in front of you without wanting the situation to be other than it is. Study the natural order of things and work with it rather than against it, for to try to change what *is* only sets up resistance... If we watch carefully, we will see that work proceeds more quickly and easily if we stop 'trying', if we stop putting in so much extra effort, if we stop looking for results."

Be like water, which is soft yet can wear down the hardest stone. Throw a rock into the water and it makes a big initial splash. But after quietly making way for it, the water quickly surrounds and swallows the stone and begins the slow process of erosion.

The rock stands fast—immobile, unbending, isolated, imposing. But because it is so rigid, it has little chance against the persistent flow of the water. Given enough time, water reduces the biggest boulder to grains of sand. Water wins in the end because it is flexible.

If there's one key prerequisite for staying active indefinitely in running, it is staying flexible—flowing like the water instead of standing firm or rolling out of control like the rock.

Flow along your own best channel.

Flow with the current instead of trying to swim upstream or trying to outrun the natural pace.

Flow around obstacles instead of trying to smash through them.

Flow on in endless cycles instead of looking for stopping places.

Flow in tune with the surroundings, but taking new life from them and giving it back. Still water stagnates and isolated streams dry and die.

As long as a stream is alive, it wants to flow. Even when it has dried to a trickle or is penned behind a dam, the potential to run— the *urge* to run—is still there. All it needs to keep running is a clear channel and strong banks to hold the water in. Natural momentum takes care of the rest.

Running is easy, so long as it stays inside of natural laws. Flowing with the current is easier on a person than standing against it. But runners get into trouble, too, when they try to go faster than they're meant to go. To make the current go faster, they add more hard miles to the stream. The added volume and force makes the flow harder to control. In extreme cases, the raging tide creeps up the banks and starts biting away at them. The banks are the foundations of good health through which running moves.

Keep adding to the load and it eventually spills over the rim, ripping through the countryside and creating assorted havoc. That's when nature steps in and puts pains in the way of free-flowing running.

The way to avoid running into these dams is to run at the rate the current wants to go. Run fast, run slow. Run shallow, run deep. Run hot, run cold. But keep running. By being persistent and flexible, few obstacles are insurmountable. Run in tune with the surroundings, realizing that your channel is already set and that most environmental conditions are beyond your control.

Constantly absorb new life from the tributaries all around, carrying it along like a relay runner into bigger and richer streams as you go. Keep running. Persist. Adapt. Absorb. Only by stopping and not starting again can you fail.

As long as you're moving, you're living, changing, growing like the river. Once you stop, you stagnate and have lost.

REFERENCES

Parts of *Run Gently, Run Long* may sound familiar to many readers who've followed *Runner's World* and the *RW* booklets through the years. A significant part of this book has appeared piecemeal in other places since 1970. All of it was written originally with this book in mind, but segments leaked into print other places as *Run Gently* eased its way toward completion.

Listed here are the places material was published earlier, along with other sources of information used. All writing is mine unless indicated otherwise.

FOREWORD
Dylan, Bob—"It's All Over Now, Baby Blue," M. Witmark and Sons, 1965.

Lao Tzu—*A Translation From Tao Te Ching,* New American Library, New York, N.Y.

CHAPTER ONE
Bach, Richard—*Jonathan Livingston Seagull,* MacMillan Co., New York, N.Y., 1970.

"Wishing He Could Fly," *Runner's World,* April 1973, p. 9.

"Steering Clear Of Bumps," *Runner's World,* March 1973, pp. 28-29.

"The Trauma Of Stopping," *Runner's World,* Oct. 1973, pp. 13-14.

"Foreword (third printing)," *LSD: The Humane Way to Train,* Tafnews Press, Los Altos, Calif., 1973.

Burfoot, Amby—"Afterword," *LSD: The Humane Way to Train,* Tafnews Press, Los Altos, Calif. 1969.

Winrow, Ed—"When Athlete Becomes Coach," *Runner's World,* Jan. 1971, pp. 52-53.

Osler, Tom—"Avoiding All Injuries," *Encyclopedia of Athletic Medicine,* pp. 18-22, World Publications, 1972.

O'Neill, Desmond—"Imperfect Shoes, Imperfect Feet," *Runner's World,* Jan. 1973, pp. 6-7.

CHAPTER TWO
Newton, Arthur—*Commonsense Athletics,* George Berridge and Co. Ltd., London, England, 1948.

"Sources of Systems," *Runner's Training Guide,* pp. 30-31, World Publications, 1973.

"Why Take Chances?" *Runner's World*, July 1973, p. 5.

Milner, Philip—"Jogger, Look To The Dog," *Midwest Magazine (Chicago Sun-Times)*, Jan. 6, 1974, pp. 15-18.

"Distance Running Scene," *Runner's World,* May 1971, pp. 36-37.

"Got That Run-Down Feeling?" *Runner's World*, Sept. 1971, pp. 36-37.

"Reading Body Signs," *Encyclopedia of Athletic Medicine,* pp. 14-15, World Publications, 1972.

"Stressing One Point," *Runner's Training Guide*, pp. 13-14, World Publications, 1973.

CHAPTER THREE

"Interview: Arthur Lydiard," *Runner's World*, July 1970, pp. 8-13.

Sheehan, George—"From The Ground Up," *Encyclopedia of Athletic Medicine,* pp. 25-26, World Publications, 1972.

"Run To Your Own Best Beat," *Runner's World*, June 1973, pp. 18-19.

"Group Therapy Each Saturday," *Runner's World,* Dec. 1973, p. 3.

Milner, Philip—"Jogger, Look To The Dog," *Midwest Magazine (Chicago Sun-Times)*, Jan. 6, 1974, pp. 15-18.

"Training Hard, the Easy Way," *Runner's World*, March 1971, pp. 36-37.

CHAPTER FOUR

"Excruciating Ecstasy," *Racing Techniques*, pp. 5-6, World Publications, 1972.

"Finding The Limits," *Practical Running Psychology*, pp. 38-39, 1972.

"Training to Compete," *Runner's World*, Sept. 1973, pp. 8-14.

CHAPTER FIVE

"To Quit Or Not To Quit?" *Runner's World*, Aug. 1973, p. 9.

"Running Like The Rivers," *Runner's World*, Aug. 1973, p. 14.

Joe Henderson, editor of Runner's World and the monthly booklet series, has earlier authored such books as "LSD—The Humane Way to Train," "Road Racers and Their Training," and
"Thoughts on the Run." Henderson was born in 1943, and
began running and writing on the sport in 1958.

Run for it...

The Complete Runner

If you run alone, with a friend or with thousands, there is something to be learned from every step you take. And to help you get the most out of your learning experience is **The Complete Runner.**

Written by runners who have spent a lifetime learning—Joe Henderson, George Sheehan, Ernst van Aaken, Kathrine Switzer, Hal Higdon and many more—**The Complete Runner** will give you insight into the realms of pleasure and pain that exist in running.

Plenty of practical information is provided. Information on a runner's diet, training, footwear, technique, physiology and psychology, along with chapters on competition, teamwork and promotion, make this the most complete volume on running ever written. 1974 Hb., second printing, 398 pp., ill., $10.95. Use the order form below to order yours today.

----------Order Form----------

Please send me _____ copies of **The Complete Runner.** Enclosed is $10.95 per copy, plus 40c postage and handling. California residents add 6% sales tax.

Name_____

Address_____

City/State/Zip_____

Runner's World
Box 366 Mtn. View, CA 94040

RUNNER'S WORLD
MAGAZINE

Run longer and more gently with **Runner's World,** the magazine for all running enthusiasts.

- Complete coverage of the most interesting and dramatic races.
- In-depth interviews and penetrating personality profiles of the key figures in the sport.
- Running shorts, racing highlights, coming events, news and views.
- Medical advice column from Dr. George Sheehan.
- Each issue is a valuable addition to your running—each is solidly packed with practical, useful, informative articles.

RUNNER'S WORLD MAGAZINE
Post Office Box 366
Mountain View, CA 94040

Please enter my subscription for the following—
_____ Renewal _____ New Subscription
_____ One Year (monthly — 12 issues) $9.50 _____ Two Years $18.00
_____ Three Years $25.50 _____ Five Years $40.00 _____ Ten Years $70.00

NAME_____

ADDRESS_____

CITY/STATE/ZIP_____

For faster service, please enclose payment